Scientific and Esoteric Encyclopedia of UFOs, Aliens and Extraterrestrial Gods

Volume II: A (Aliens)

*** *** ***

Maximillien de Lafayette

Volume II

SCIENTIFIC AND ESOTERIC ENCYCLOPEDIA OF UFOS, ALIENS AND EXTRATERRESTRIAL GODS

The world's first and most authoritative encyclopedia of its kind!!

Published in the United States of America and Germany.

Printed by Times Square Press. New York.
Date of Publication: June 27, 2014.

Scientific and Esoteric Encyclopedia of UFOs, Aliens and Extraterrestrial Gods

Volume II: A (Aliens) from a set of 20 volumes.

Maximillien de Lafayette

*** *** ***

Times Square Press
New York Berlin Paris Madrid
2014

Table Of Contents

- Excerpts from other meetings with aliens which occurred years later.
- Habitable planet or an Earth-like planet.
- Earth is the universe's dumpster.
- Aliens' reproduction and the "Productive Essence".
- Manufactured aliens
- Aliens' Transcripts (AT).
- A file from the Aliens' Transcripts which was shared with NASA, USAF, The White House, and NSA.
- Addendum to the Aliens' Transcripts.
- On Jesus, the 4 Bibles and Dark Matter.
- Universal Energy and Dark Matter.
- Locations of negative energy on planet Earth.
- Who reviewed the Addendum to the transcripts?

*** *** ***

A

Continued from Volume I

Aliens: Intelligent species or races which are not human in nature, and are from an unknown origin. They include both the extraterrestrials and the intraterrestrials.

Aliens, contact/communication with:
1-What should we do in the event they do contact us?
"It depends on the race that communicates with you or suddenly appears in your world. If they are hostile, there is nothing you can do about it because they are far more advanced than you. It would be a bad day for earth.

It is not advisable for your kind to try to communicate with other species, for your own safety..." told us an alien during an initial meeting that occurred in 1947. The alien added, "It is best not to try to contact any of the other species because you cannot be sure who you may come into contact with. You may find yourself contacting a race that has hostile tendencies."

Numerous scientists were concerned with the possibility of the arrival of aggressive extraterrestrials. They were referring to some alien races they did not meet with. They feared the "Unknown."

Dr. Teller reassured the military and President Harry Truman that the aliens he knew were not a threat to us, on the contrary, if well-handled, they could become a "formidable asset" he said.

Many disagreed.

Ironically, some sixty years later, Stephen Hawking suggested that extraterrestrials are almost certain to exist — but that instead of seeking them out, humanity should be doing all it that can to avoid any contact.

"To my mathematical brain, the numbers alone make thinking about aliens perfectly rational," he said. "The real challenge is to work out what aliens might actually be like."

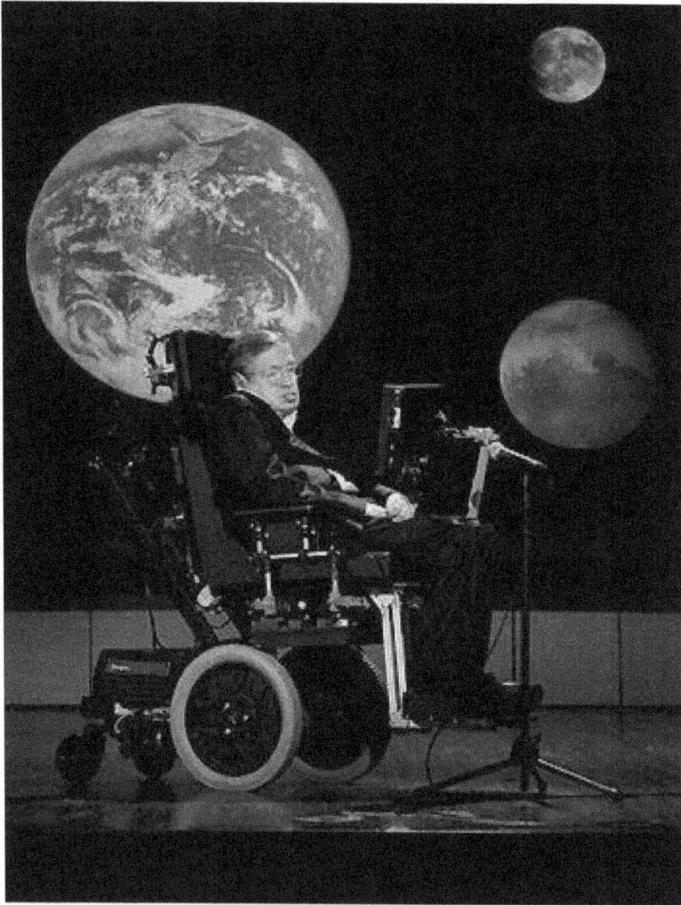

Stephen Hawking

One scene from his documentary for the Discovery Channel shows herds of two-legged herbivores browsing on an alien cliff-face where they are picked off by flying, yellow lizard-like predators.

Another shows glowing fluorescent aquatic animals forming vast shoals in the oceans thought to underlie the thick ice coating Europa, one of the moons of Jupiter.

Such scenes are speculative, but Hawking uses them to lead on to a serious point: that a few life forms could be intelligent and pose a threat. Hawking believes that contact with such a species could be devastating for humanity. He suggests that aliens might simply raid Earth for its resources and then move on: "We only have to look at ourselves to see how intelligent life might develop into something we wouldn't want to meet. I imagine they might exist in massive ships, having used up all the resources from their home planet.

Such advanced aliens would perhaps become nomads, looking to conquer and colonise whatever planets they can reach." He concludes that trying to make contact with alien races is "a little too risky".

He said: "If aliens ever visit us, I think the outcome would be much as when Christopher Columbus first landed in America, which didn't turn out very well for the Native Americans." –The Sunday Times, April 25, 2010. Because alien life might not have DNA like us, Hawking warned: "Watch out if you would meet an alien. You could be infected with a disease with which you have no resistance."-Fox News.

2-So, why some aliens are here? What made them come?
Because the aliens are "on our way", meaning that Earth and our solar system and their location/position in the Milky Way, are their passage to other galaxies. This of course applies only to out of space aliens; simply put, extraterrestrials.

The intraterrestrials are here, simply because they live on Earth. They have inhabited planet Earth for millions of years.

More on this point in other parts of the book.

The aliens (From different worlds and dimensions) were here before, and have visited planet Earth occasionally, but not for the reasons given by some colorful ufologists, abductees, contactees, channelers and New Age enthusiasts.

Extraterrestrials did not come to Earth to mine for gold, enslave humans, or to give a message of love, hope and salvation to a few "chosen ones." They are not our celestial brothers and sisters as many psychics and spiritual healers think, or want us to believe. Extraterrestrials are scientific entities/manifestations, and not spiritual messengers.

And in many instances, the UFOs people we see in the sky are alien spacecrafts created by intraterrestrials; some are piloted by the Grays, and some are of a robotic nature.

If an extraterrestrial message of an extreme importance is to be given to humanity, aliens would simply reveal it to all of us and use a scientific method of communication/delivery.

3-Telepathy is not the only method of communication.
Contrary to a general belief, the Grays-Aliens do not always communicate with us, (especially with abductees and contactees) telepathically. Many of them are capable of speaking in English.

This was confirmed by official reports and documented in the Aliens Transcripts.

4-Telepathic communication between the Grays (Greys) aliens and contactees and abductees:
The alleged telepathic communication that occurred between an alien intraterrestrial and so-called contactees and abductees is a very rare phenomenon. It only occurs when the individual is an exceptionally alert person, who remains coherent, and does not succumb to panic and emotional disturbances, and does not fall into a state of paralysis.

5-No personal messages from aliens:
Aliens and intraterrestrials do not give individuals, and so-called contactees and abductees, personal messages to be delivered to humanity. Aliens and intraterrestrials rarely talk to abductees, almost never; no reason to.

In some rare instances, they express "something" by slowly and gradually raising their hands or directly staring at individuals, who are usually in a state of shock, fear, confusion, and paralysis.

6-Galactic languages:
Not all aliens have the same vocabulary. There are millions of galactic languages and dialects.
However, there is a universal/cosmic protocol language used and understood by millions of galactic civilizations.

7-Communicating with an alien during a meeting:
Throughout the entire meeting the United States military and scientists had with an alien, the alien was not communicating verbally; no sound was heard from her. Her communication was directly transmitted from her brain (cellular motor) to the device she gave us.
The device would receive her thoughts and answers in colors, images, frequencies, and dots like we use to send messages through the Morse code.
At the far end of the machine, there is a screen which displayed dots, multiple dots, empty spaces, and slashes and deciphered the letters and forms.
Secondly, after this was displayed on the screen, the machine would talk to us in English, in a very and most unusual English vocabulary. For example, the alien never used pronouns, such as "I" and occasionally she would use "we".
The alien never said we have a body; instead she said we have an Essence. It took the military quite a while to re-interpret her English into their English. And, quite often they missed the point.
A major part of her mind transmission was lost in the translation.
Later on the military decided firmly that top notch linguists in the country should be present at all meetings with aliens.
Hopefully to help translate and interpret the alien languages and expressions correctly.
Weeks later, I discovered that this was absolutely true because the alien device contained a limited amount of English vocabulary.
And the words used mentally by the alien, technologically transmitted and displayed by the machine were those often used by the military in their daily life- normal everyday slang. It was very obvious, to me, that all her answers were not given to us with technological and scientific terms. At one point the female alien told us she avoided that on purpose.

17

8-On how extraterrestrials and/or aliens communicate with each other:
The following is an excerpt from the "Aliens Transcripts" 1947-1948
Question: Do you communicate with all (Other extraterrestrials) of them?
Alien: Yes.
Question: So, how do you communicate with all of them?
Alien: In many different ways.
We use our cellular motor. Messages and communications are sent and received via images projected mentally, graphs, mind transmission channels, and collective transmission.

9-Talking to extraterrestrials:
Anunnaki and extraterrestrials have no intention whatsoever in engaging into a dialogue with ordinary human beings. If they have an agenda, and/or are on a mission, they either abduct (Not the Anunnaki) humans, or directly contact scientists working with them in secret facilities, laboratories and bases.
Anunnaki do not talk tête-à-tête with humans, nor convey their messages on a personal basis. And most certainly, Anunnaki do not abduct humans. However, direct and personal contact did happen with aliens. They were the "Greys".
But this occurrence is extremely rare. Ulema Al Bakri said: "And when and if it happens, extraterrestrials would not pronounce one word and walk away, or stutter as some contactees reported", including one famous contactee in Switzerland who made headlines worldwide and became the messenger of the Lyrans on earth.
When aliens contact (So to speak) or encounter a human being, they usually complete sentences and engage into a dialogue, even though, as it was reported, the dialogue is short, and their words are incomprehensible, and the voice is mechanic and fuzzy.
In some instances, the aliens transmit their messages mentally, not telepathically, because for the telepathic phenomenon to occur, you need two telepathic people, and most certainly contactees who are regular folks are neither gifted nor trained telepaths.

You cannot talk to another person on your cellular phone, if the other party does not have one.
Do you want to try?
Same thing applies to telepathy; it needs two telepathic stations, fully operational and fully capable of sending and receiving messages.

The human brain did not yet reach this level. Although some preliminary forms of telepathy between humans were noticed in rare instances. Extraterrestrials are capable of speaking and understanding many languages, including our own.
They assimilate and "compute" words, sentences and physical expressions with mathematical formulas and numerical values.
Some extraterrestrials have limited vocal chords capabilities, but they can very quickly acquire additional vocal faculties, and earth dialects by rewinding sounds and vibes.

Contrary to what many contactees and others claim or depict, extraterrestrials from higher dimensions/spheres do not talk like computerized machines.
They have their own language but also they can absorb and assimilate all the languages on earth in a blink of an eye via the reception and emission of a spatial memory.

Aliens and extraterrestrials, meetings with:
The first meeting with aliens was a pre-scheduled and agreed upon event. The aliens told us where and when they will meet with us, and the military approved.
According to notes from the Aliens Transcripts (AT), Section 9: Addendum 12-Briefing 341-E1, 1947, this first meeting was arranged by an alien who was in the custody of the United States Air Force.
At the bottom of the page, there is an arrow and a reference made to a certain "Lt. Colonel S..." who coordinated the meeting. On the next page, top left, one could read the following: "No outfits", which means that those who waited for the arrival of the aliens did not wear any particular suits or protective suits.

19

The alien who arranged the meeting:
The alien who arranged the meeting between our government and the extraterrestrials and aliens stayed at a military base for approximately 3 months and 4 days, and later died.
Her body was sent to a military hospital.
The alien was captured after her spacecraft crashed, for missing to "jump" into the time-space pocket, needed to enter and exit a physical dimension. The three other aliens died on impact. The one who survived was a female alien-hybrid, although no genital organs were visible.

Generalities: General assembly in the initial meetings.
Representatives from governments' agencies (Military and civilian) in the Eastern and Western Hemispheres met several times with aliens, intraterrestrials and extraterrestrials in many places, on military bases, in the desert, underwater, in foreign countries, in the United States, around Earth's orbit, and outer-space.
High echelon/top brass in the military (Army, Navy, Air Force), nations' very best scientists, codes decipherers and breakers, and "select" linguists working for governments and semi-official organizations attended these meetings.
In some meetings, members of the clergy (Catholic Church) and a very prominent Protestant preacher were present.
Numerous briefings of rapports with aliens and aliens' transcripts are well preserved in secret vaults. The United States government met with different aliens races on many occasions. And the spectrum of the discussions is ad infinitum.

Meeting with three different non-human species:
Our governments met with three different non-human species with an exceptional intelligence, and highly advanced technology and science:
- a-An intraterrestrial non-human race called the Greys or Grays.
- b-The Anunnaki.
- c-Naftarian or Naftarim.

Organism structure of various aliens' races:

In the original (First report) report on an alien, which also contained "medical observations", it was noted that the surviving alien has no gender.

Later on, in a communiqué sent to the Pentagon, the surviving alien's gender was acknowledged as a male; however no genital organs were visible.

The story is getting more complicated, because rumors start to circulate that the alien was a female indeed, because herself told them about her gender.

I tend to believe that the surviving alien was de facto a female; a hybrid-female, not totally Gray.

Following an autopsy conducted on the aliens' dead bodies, two medical examiners came to an astonishing conclusion:

- 1-The aliens had no lungs.
- 2-The aliens had no digestive system.
- 3-The aliens had a green color blood.
- 4-The aliens had no retina.
- 5-The aliens had no genitals. This item was mentioned twice in the Aliens Transcripts
- 6-The aliens had no vocal chords.
- 7-The aliens had three fingers on each hand.
- 8-Aliens' skin is covered with small pores that have multiple functions and purposes we do not fully understand.
- 9-The size of their brains was extremely large *par rapport* to the size of their skull.
- 10-The aliens suits were "glued" to their bodies, as if the suits were part of their skin. And much more.

Not all aliens are alike:

Not all aliens are short with three fingers on each hand. On some planets, galactic beings do not have fingers at all, not even hands. Many of our human body features and organs are useless on other planets. Eyes, hands, fingers and our five senses are not needed.

21

The intraterrestrials who originally came from Zeta Reticuli, millions of years ago told us that "not all aliens look alike. Some don't have eyes, others don't have ears, and a great number of them don't have hands, lungs and body organs similar to yours. On their planets, ears, eyes, hands and lungs are useless."-Source: The Aliens Transcripts, 1947.

The Grays-Aliens who died in the UFO crash near Roswell did not have internal organs similar to ours; they had no heart, no blood circulatory system, no mouth, no ears, etc.
And we have found from autopsy of dead aliens that they had a bizarre green liquid inside their bodies.
Some experts in the field claimed that the green fluid substituted for blood, but such claim was never confirmed by mainstream science and medical sciences.
None of the aliens who met with us had reproductive organs, a human respiratory system, and a digestive system. All of them told us that they do not consume food, and do not have waste inside their bodies, except an Anunnaki who said that her race consumes human and non-human food, but they dispose of the waste through skin pores.
The internal structure of the aliens' bodies is animated by a cellular motor located in the brain.
And the brain is neither biological nor organic.
Their brain is purely cellular consisting of intricate cells channels and mental-electrical frequencies circuit. The aliens' brain does not produce emotions, but it recognizes them as mental images.
The aliens do not have a nervous system. Thus, they do not feel pain, stress, anxiety, fatigue, hunger, heat, cold, and similar reaction and feelings.
The intraterrestrials have three long and skinny fingers on each hand. The non-human races from Ashtari and Naftari have five fingers on each hand, just like us.
Four other galactic species including the Anunnaki and Igigi resemble humans to a certain degree.
None of the aliens we have met had a retina.

Aliens from highly advanced civilizations have multiple copies of their "Essences" (Body frame, being, mental-physical structure, etc.)
In other words, authentic copies of their bodies with astonishing space-time memory capabilities.

The brain's cell is responsible for everything:
The aliens told us that about a cell in our brains (not discovered yet by science,) which is responsible for everything and anything that shapes and conditions our psyche, organism, intelligence, and SOUL.
It is in that particular cell, that the so-called HUMAN SOUL exists, lives, and transforms itself into other substances and dimensions during our life, and in the afterlife.

Aliens and extraterrestrials are built differently from us.
Note: The following was displayed on the "Voice Box Screen"; a machine the aliens gave us, and which allowed us to record and translate anything that has been said by the aliens.
Worth mentioning here that a great deal of what the alien has said was lost in the translation, simply because:
1-The vocabulary as stored in the machine was very limited;
2-The aliens' vocabulary (Words and sentences) seemed bizarre to the military interpreters and civilian linguists, because the meaning of chosen words by the alien could not be adequately translated in any of our languages;
3-Alien's technical words and scientific explanation pertaining to spacecrafts' mode of operation and construction, the nature and structural organism of the bodies of the aliens, and the world (Dimensions, zones, planets, galaxies) the aliens lived in, defied our laws of physics.

Alien: Emotions are not wired to our cellular motor.
In a meeting with aliens that occurred in 1947, in the United States of America, an extraterrestrial told us: "We don't have lungs. We don't have abdomen. We don't eat. We don't have a digestive system.

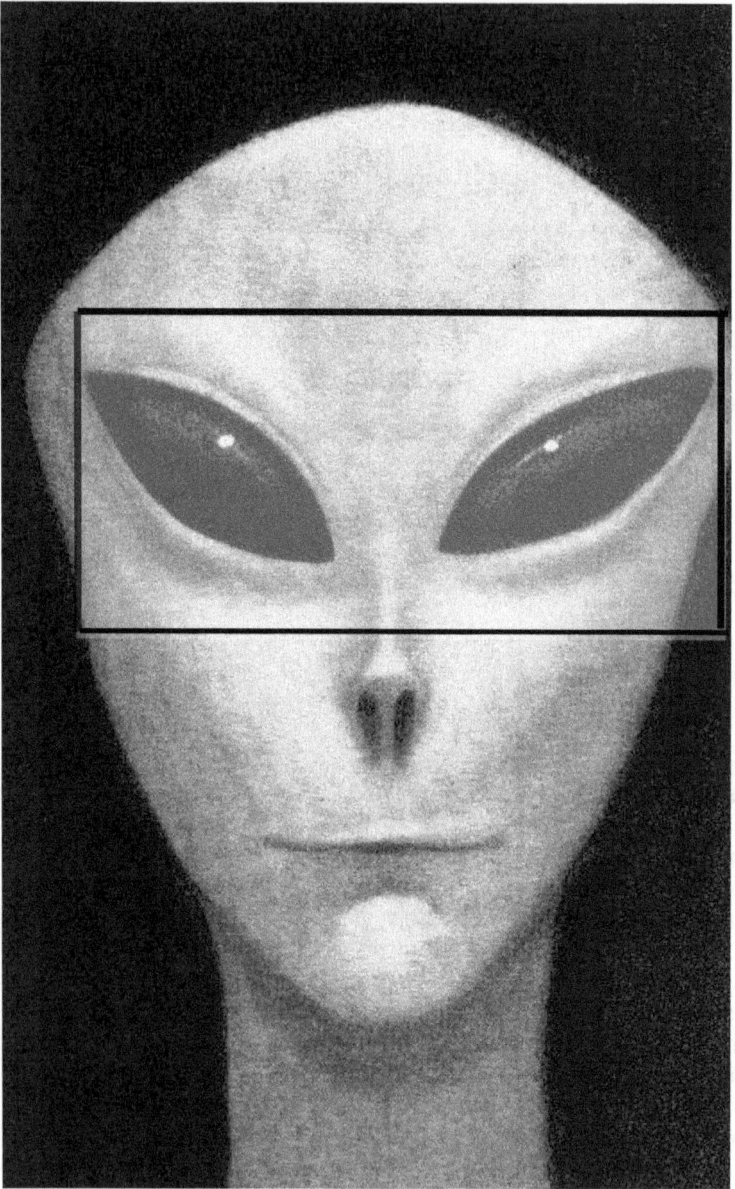

These black eyes are in fact lenses. The aliens remove them at will. They are attached to a gland we do not have in our system. The aliens don't have a retina; they see through cells channel in their brain. Three of the major functions of the lenses are:
a-Protection,
b-Navigation/direction,
c-Communication.

We don't produce waste.
We don't feel pain because we don't have a nervous system.
Emotions —as you call it – are not wired to our cellular motor.
Your kind needs emotions to express physically what you feel.
In our case, we do not show emotions, not because we don't have emotions, but because we are not a physical creation.
Our emotions are not physical, they are mental. This makes a big difference between us and you; you are physical and we are non physical. You live in a physical world, we live in time world.
Our brain operates our physical body on all levels.
When you look at me, you simply see is a frame.
I can leave it here, and go somewhere else, and continue to be myself in other places.
It will disintegrate gradually on its own, and I continue as an Essence somewhere else.
I can keep doing this endlessly."

Alien: "I start anew with another copy of my body."
A military scientist asked the alien: "So when you want to return, do you pick up with the same body?
The alien said: "If it is not harmed. If it disintegrates, then I start anew with another copy of my body. And you will not notice the difference.
The body you are now looking at could be one of my multiple copies. How would you know?
My body disintegrates only when it is harmed. But, our essence survives and continues somewhere else. The essence does not disintegrate; it continues to live in other dimensions. And within each dimension beyond the physical world there are dimensions which are created by each one of us on a mental level, and created by the cosmic energy on a physical level.
We have the power to create universes from the energy of our cellular motor.

We are very powerful, extremely advanced and we have seen so many different universes that exist or will exist in what you call the future. There is a frontier when you cross it, you will see a great number of dimensions each one entering and exiting the other.

25

The essence (the alien meant what we call, the human body or human life) also can enter and exit several dimensions instantly and simultaneously.
The Essences are multi-dimensional and vibrational essences.
They can be both physical and mental."

Alien: "We continue to exist through multiplication of ourselves."

One of the scientists who attended the meeting asked:
"Does one copy of yourself mirror or react to another?
And, does one have a direct impact on the other?
Please explain?"
The alien answered: We continue to exist through multiplication of ourselves.
The alien was asked: "Then what?"
The alien replied: "Everything you have on earth we have it and nothing of what we have, you have on earth, because we live concurrently in a physical world and a purely mental world.
Your kind lives only in a physical world.
Few thousand creatures live on different planets that have needs similar to yours, such as air, oxygen and food. And there are billions and billions of Essences who do not need what you need, like water, air and food, because they are not made from flesh and bones.
Since we do not have circulatory system, blood circulation, we don't need the organ you call heart. And since our Essence does not have tissues and muscles, no nutrition is necessary, no food is required, no water is required to keep us functioning and growing.
Our Essence is a perfect and a very powerful machine which has consciousness, fairness and extremely developed intelligence.
We are an intelligent mechanism, very peaceful, very alert, very knowledgeable of the universe, and we are also very familiar with your kind and your origin."

Alien: "We don't have waste in our bodies."

Excerpts from a transcript of a meeting with an extraterrestrial:
The alien said: "We are pure. We don't have waste in our bodies.
We do not smell. We do not bleed. We do not feel pain.

We do not feel cold. We do not feel the heat. All of those are a sign of weakness and imperfection that your kind will suffer from forever.

The difference between you and us is enormous.

Your body and our Essence are both machines.

Your kind (Human machine) is destructive and self destructive.

We are peaceful, powerful and very intelligent machine.

Your brain is weak. It is not yet fully operational. We begin to exist with a fully operationally cellular motor which has all the knowledge and information each one of us needs. Your body as a machine is made from skin, flesh, bones, and nerves.

Our essence has nothing of that.

This is why we can last for hundreds of thousands of years. Our Essence is constantly reconditioned. The body (Frame) in any of its forms self adjusts, rewinds itself and starts anew."

Extraterrestrials manufacture themselves, and are born fully grown and mature.

An extraterrestrial told us that their Essence (Being, creature) is given life and "maturity" instantly, meaning that they are born (Produced) complete. And extraterrestrial children don't have to wait long to be fully developed. They come into existence fully grown.

The extraterrestrial added, "In many dimensions, time does not exist, therefore it's not necessary for a new born essence (creature) to wait for many years to grow up to be an adult or mature person. There is no time outside your world.

In our dimensions, we don't have age reference because no one grows older than others. We stay the same forever."

Smell (Odor) of aliens' bodies:

Aliens' bodies do not have body odors. Only, when the body of an intraterrestrial or a hybrid has been autopsied, a very strong and suffocating smell comes out from inside the body.

Usually, it comes out, when a green fluid suddenly emerges from the internal organs which are extremely different from ours.

None of the operating surgeons and nurses inside the autopsy room could stand the smell.

They ran away "like a mad dog" said one of the military nurses. In fact, the odor was so strong, it invaded the whole compound. They had to seal the room for 24 hours. Physicians at Water Reed Army Medical Center, became very concerned and alarmed, for they sought that the smell could be very toxic.

Note: Worth mentioning here that no autopsy report from Walter Reed was ever issued by a physician (Pathologist) who conducted any kind of autopsy on dead aliens.
Instead, scattered and reconstructed medical notes (Unsigned) were sent to the Pentagon two days later.
This is not a normal military or medical procedure as any one might guess. But it did happen intentionally, and I am unable to elaborate further on this situation.

The names of the pathologists and assisting nurses were never revealed to "outsider-civilians". And the preliminary notes vanished from the face of the earth. Thus, there is no way to honestly and accurately document the autopsy.
And most certainly, the autopsy was not filmed.
I am absolutely certain that no civilian or any officer below the rank of Colonel had access to any autopsy report. Even at the Pentagon, only two generals and one military surgeon had access to a medical report describing in details the anatomy and physiology of the aliens. Said report was then submitted to The White House.
An insider said, "To the best of my knowledge, there is only one original report which remained hidden somewhere in a secret military dossier at The Pentagon, and one copy of the report which was read by the President and YES disposed of. Grosso modo, and quite honestly, we don't know a thing about the aliens' autopsy. Yes, it did happen, but there are no records to substantiate the fact that it did happen."

Words "sex" and "intercourse":
The words "sex" and "intercourse" do not exist in the aliens' vocabulary.

Not even once, any of these two words were ever used by an alien during any meeting.
Yet, the aliens are very familiar with how we reproduce and how human sexual behavior conditions and influences our lifestyle and habits.

Aliens could not walk straight:
The aliens we met could not walk straight and in a balanced manner, because they did not have muscles to support their weight, even though, they were very miniscule and frail.
Nevertheless their hands were very flexible and agile. Only two species could walk gracefully; the Anunnaki and the Naftarians. The hybrids walked just like us. And some were tall by aliens' standards. However, they could not move their head right and left without twisting their body. It appeared to us as if their neck was barely attached to their head.
This is one of the easily recognized characteristic features of the Grays-Hybrids.

Aliens' faculties and brain:
To entities on other planets and multi-dimensional zones, eyes like ours are not needed, for they use different organs to see; some use skins pores, others cells in the brain. And the brain (Cellular Motor) is not necessary located inside a skull; it could be found anywhere under the skin, or on the surface, even stored in a collective awareness.

No sense of time:
They Grays have no sense of time. However, they can clearly differentiate between past events and future events. They do not follow any chronological order or time-frame sequences.

The Grays are claustrophobic:
The Grays are claustrophobic. They will be disoriented if they are confined in a small area for a long period of time in the same place.

How old are the extraterrestrials?

29

As old as the Universe itself; as old as the cosmic energy because everything is made from the cosmic energy.

Their Essence (Structure/Organism) never dies physically or mentally, it is transformed and re-transformed endlessly.

This concept is not new. Antoine-Laurent de Lavoisier (August 26, 1743 - May 8, 1794) already said, "Rien ne se perd, rien ne se crée, tout se transforme", (Nothing is lost, nothing is created, everything is transformed) based upon the famous statement of Anaxagore de Clazomenes' "Rien ne naît ni ne périt, mais des choses déjà existantes se combinent, puis se séparent de nouveau." (Nothing is born or perished, but things that they already exist, combine and separate again.)

Lavoisier and his wife in 1788. Painting by David.

What is their average life-span?
It depends on each civilization; some are constantly superposed, multiplied and reproduced. Some live millions of years, others hundreds of thousands of years.
It all depends on the level of their development, advancement, technology and cosmic awareness. Extraterrestrials who are an essential part of the cosmic particles never die.

Nature/substance of alien races:
- Entities without a Frame (physical structure).
- Cellular
- Purely mental
- Ethero-organic
- Vibrational
- Multi-dimensional
- Some are physical
- Physical-mental
- Superposed presences
- Some exist between parallel dimensions
- Some are from the future
- Some did not exist yet
- Penetrating vibrations
- Organic
- Spheric
- Some have all our physical senses and faculties but do not have ears to hear, eyes to see, mouths to taste, hands to feel because those organs are completely useless outside our world.
- And some your mind cannot understand.

Three major races of aliens:
Note: Some have claimed that the United States government had numerous meetings with the extraterrestrial Nordics and Lyrans (Lyrians). It is possible, but I had no access to files that could substantiate such claim.

Worth mentioning here that files on extraterrestrials and intraterrestrials are never shared in their entirety with all the government's agencies and branches dealing with the alien phenomenon. What the NSA has on aliens is not necessarily shared by the FBI. And what the CIA has in its files on aliens' operations is not ipso facto known to the United States Air Force, so on.

Race 1: An intraterrestrial non-human.
This is a race of aliens with highly advanced and sophisticated intelligence, who have lived on Earth for millions of years.
Originally from Zeta Reticuli, this race is known to the general public as the Greys or the Grays; a reference or possibly a descriptive definition given by people who claimed that they have been abducted by the Grays, and/or have encountered them. Official records refer to aliens as Biological Entities, Space Monkeys, Shorty Aliens, EBE, Aliens.
They were called intra-terrestrials because they have their habitats "inside the Earth", underwater, as well as on remote areas inaccessible to us.
They were mentioned numerous times in the Aliens Transcripts.
The genetic breed they created, known as the hybrids live with them in their habitats underwater, as well as on land in remote areas. Many hybrid children were adopted by human families who have a perfectly normal life. The intraterrestrials are the ones who pilot the UFOs and the USOs.

Race 2: The Anunnaki.
They are wrongly defined as those who came to Earth from above, referring to Nibiru, their home planet.
The Anunnaki were the deities worshipped by the Sumerians and Akkadians in Mesopotamia. They are of an extraterrestrial origin, but did not come from Nibiru, which is an Akkadian and a Chaldean name for Jupiter. Their constellation is called Ashta.Ri (Aldebaran). Our governments met only twice with the Anunnaki who were interestingly enough, represented by two females.
This race was mentioned 14 times in the Aliens Transcripts.

32

The word Anunnaki is a Sumerian/Akkadian/Assyrian/Chaldean noun. It is composed of two words:

a-Anunna, which means the entirety of the gods (All the gods and goddesses of Mesopotamia).

b-Ki, which means Earth, and the underworld, the netherworld, and the world of death.

Thus, the correct definition of the word Anunnnaki is: Gods of Earth and/or gods of the underworld.

The Akkadian/Sumerian Anunnaki word is used in a plural form to represent the deities of heaven and Earth, called Anunna in Sumerian and Akkadian.

Later on in history, and in order to differentiate between the Anunnaki and the Igigi, the scribes called the Anunnaki, the gods of Earth (Ki), also gods of the netherworld, and the Igigi, gods of heaven. This differentiation is very clear in all the Mesopotamian clay tablets, particularly in the Ishtar Descent to the Underworld (Ki), the poem/myth of Gilgamesh, the Enuma Elish, etc...

Other names for the Anunnaki:

The Anunnaki were known to many neighboring countries in the Near East, Middle East, and Anatolia.

And because of the languages' differences, the Anunnaki were called differently.

For instance:

1- The Habiru (Early Hebrews/Israelites) called them Nephilim, meaning to fall down to earth, as well as Anakim and Raphaim. Some passages in the Old Testament refer to them as Elohim.

2- In Assyrian-Chaldean, and Syriac-Aramaic, the Anunnaki are called Jabaariyn, meaning the mighty ones.

3- In some Aramaic, Chaldean and Hebrew texts, the Anunnaki are called Gibborim, which means the mighty or majestic ones. Jababira in literary Arabic.

4- The Egyptians called them Neteru.

5- The Greeks called them the Annodoti.

6- In the Book of Enoch, they are called B'nai Elohim (Children of God), the Nephilim, and the "Watchers".

According to some linguists, the word Anunnaki is a loan word from the Sumerian word A.nun "n-a-k", meaning literarily:

a-Semen/descendants of the (Ak) monarch (Nun) and refers to the offspring of the king of heaven An/Anum.

As a group of Akkadian and Sumerian deities, quite often, the Anunnaki were associated with the Anunna, meaning the fifty great gods. Anuna was written in various forms, such as:

a-A-nun-na,

b-Anu-na,

c-Anuma-ki-ni,

d-Anu-na-ki.

Various attributes or definitions were given to them, such as:

a-Major gods in comparison to the Igigi who were considered minor gods.

b-Those of a royal blood or ancestry.

c-The royal offspring,

d-The great gods of heaven and earth. An means heaven, and ki means earth.

Race 3: Naftarian.

This race, and sometimes called Naftarim came from the star system of Naftari, yet to be discovered and acknowledged by mainstream science. Official records show that our governments did meet with the Naftarians on many occasions for a very long time. And the first meeting occurred in 1947.

The Naftarim were mentioned numerous times in the Aliens Transcripts, because of the vital scientific information and instructions we received from them. Some were extremely useful to us because of the information they gave us in our attempts to reverse alien technology.

Catalogue of various categories of extraterrestrials and alien races:

The United States and Russia have huge dossiers cataloguing alien species under different categories, such as, to name a few:

- a-Category
- b-Nature
- c-Physiognomy
- d-Location of their habitat

- e-Faculty
- f-Intelligence
- g-Science
- h-Technology
- i-Crafts
- j-Communication
- k-Joint programs

France, United Kingdom, Russia, Germany and the United States governments have an illustrated catalogue of various categories of non-human, extraterrestrial and alien races who are scattered in the immensity of the Cosmos, and some who live on Earth.

The drawings and illustrations of their anatomy, physiology and physiognomy were based upon information given to us by the Grays.

Our knowledge of outer-space entities comes directly from the Grays, and a lengthy report from an Anunnaki.

So far, none of these extraterrestrial entities contacted us. We do not have sufficient or meaningful information and scientific data about any of them. Some, for reasons we don't know or we don't understand, have visited planet Earth, thousands of years ago, and never returned.

According to aliens we met with, galactic civilizations are not interested in us, as simple as that.

Why? Because they are millions of years ahead of us, and we have nothing to offer them.

*** *** ***

Aliens/Grays-Government Meetings

Belgium	0	0	0
Brazil	0	0	0
China	0	0	0
Japan	0	0	0
France	0	0	0
Israel	0	0	0
Mexico	2		
Russia	1	Military Base	1948
Russia	2	Military Base	1949
Russia	3	Kapustin Yar	1961
Russia		Ibid	1980
USA	2	Military Base	1947
USA	3	Military Base	1948
USA	6	Ibid	1954-1958
USA	Permanent	Permanent	1974-Present
USA	Joint Programs	Outer-space	1979-2000
USA	Training	Mexico	2000-2002
USA	Technology	Military Bases	Permanent
USA	Permanent	Bases on Earth	1959-Present
USA	1	Space	Undisclosed
USA	1	Space	Undisclosed

Briefings and Transcripts of Aliens/Grays-Government Meetings

Belgium	0	0	0
Brazil	0	0	0
China	0	0	0
Japan	0	0	0
France	0	0	0
Israel	0	0	0
Mexico	96	76	81
Russia	1,200	2,100	432
USA	28,000	3,600	3,400

★★★　★★★　★★★

Complex machines were used by the aliens to talk to us.
In the first two meetings, very complicated and complex tools/machines were used by the aliens to talk to us. The aliens carried with them a special device in a circular metallic box (Voice-box, also called VB); they had two different kinds of boxes they used in communicating with us. Later on, the aliens began to speak to us in English and Russian, with a perfect accent, respectively.

In the second meeting, the aliens gave us the Translation Signals Box (TSB), which allowed us to respond to their communications and messages.

Later on, the CTF (Transmission Channel), originally "Channel of the transmissions frequency of aliens" was used. Contrary to a general belief, the aliens did not talk to us telepathically. On their device, they had the recordings of all the languages and dialects of Earth, including versions of their own languages.

But they have never communicated with us using their own languages, for the device they used to communicate with us was especially designed for this purpose.

Protective suits:
In the first meeting, military men and civilians did not wear protective suits as it was claimed by some.
So, apparently, the aliens did something to their spacecrafts, so radiations emitted by their ships would not affect us. It was later explained to us that they totally eliminated radioactive emission of their crafts to prevent any damages and injuries to the bodies and brains of those who were waiting for their arrival.
However, in other cases and situations, when aliens do not announce their arrival or landing, their crafts emit and leave behind radioactive radiations.
If strong enough, the radiations would cause severe burns and serious damage to our brain, body molecules, cells, and organs.
The aliens were wearing protective suits. They told us, human germs cause them skin irritations and dermatologic allergy.
This is one of the reasons they wear those silver-metallic suits and eyes-protection-screen-glasses.
Others reasons are, to name a few:
- a-Countering anti-gravity inside their ships,
- b-Protection against G caused by sharp turns and sudden entering-exiting time-space pockets (Speed of light)
- c-Navigation purposes,
- d-"Zooming into" the mind of humans,
- e-Thoughts projection
- f-Mental holography,
- g-Communication, so on...

The aliens told us to warn our people not to come close to any of their spacecrafts when they land unannounced (In all cases and circumstances), because their spacecrafts' radiations cause:
- a-Temporary loss of memory,
- b-Nausea,
- c-Extensive vomiting,

- d-Severe headaches,
- e-Temporary paralysis,
- f-Temporary loss of sight,
- g-Severe skin burns, so on...

Who were present at the meetings*?
Military men
Scientists
Photographers
Psychics
Code breakers
Linguists
Intelligence and national security agents
Test pilots
Propulsion system experts and engineers
Pathologists
Astrophysicists
Futurists
Physicians
Psychologists
Psychiatrists
Nuclear physicists
*Note: This constitutes the general assembly in the initial meetings. Many attendees were removed by the military from forthcoming meetings with aliens.

Copies of the reports and transcripts of the meetings:
- Transcripts were sent in duplicate copies to The White House on Monday 9, February 1948.
- A synopsis of the transcripts (Heavily censored) sent to Dr. ...on Thursday 26, February 1948.
- A Top Secret Presidential Memorandum (Order) was issued on: Wednesday 18, February 1948.
- A follow-up report was written and sent to The White House by Dr. Von Braun and Dr. Teller on: Thursday 26, February 1948.

Who reviewed the transcripts of the meetings?

Names of some scientists, military men and others who reviewed the Alien-Meeting Transcripts and commented upon, (To name a few):

- General Kenney. Commander of the United States Strategic Air Forces.
- Kenneth C. Royall. Special Assistant to the Secretary of War, 1945. Under Secretary of War, 1945-1947. Secretary of War, 1947. Secretary of the Army, 1947-1949.
- Dr. Peter Goldmark (Péter Károly Goldmark). Scientist, inventor, and recipient of the National Medal of Science, awarded by President Carter.
- General Curtis LeMay, Commander-in-Chief of the Strategic Air Command, from1948 to1957, and Vice Chief of Staff, U.S. Air Force, from 1957 to 1961.
- Major General Clements McMullen, Commanding General of the San Antonio Air Materiel Area, Kelly Air Force Base, San Antonio, Texas.
- Major General St. Clair Streett, special assistant to the Commanding General, Air Materiel Command.
- John Bardeen. Physicist and inventor of the Transistor. He won twice the Noble Prize in Physics.
- Mr. Warren R. Austin.
- Secretary of Defense Forrestal.
- Dr. W. Albert Noyes, President of the American Chemical Society.
- Dr. Edward Teller, father of the H Bomb.
- Dr. von Braun.
- Dr. Enrico Fermi, winner of the Nobel Prize in physics. In 1938, Dr. Fermi was the world's greatest expert on neutrons.
- Dr. Vannevar Bush. Vice-president and dean at MIT in 1932. President of Carnegie Institute in 1939. Chairman of the National Advisory Committee for Aeronautics. President Roosevelt appointed him Chairman of the National Defense Resource Committee (NDRC). FDR's senior military research advisor.

- General Nathan F. Twining, United States Air Force Chief of Staff.
- Lt. General Arthur Gilbert Trudeau, Chief of the Army's Research and Development Command.
- Rear Admiral Roscoe H. Hillenkoetter, the first CIA Director, Director of the Central Intelligence Group, Member of the board of governors of the National Investigations Committee on Aerial Phenomena, etc.
- President George Bush, Sr.
- A scientist from Kelley-Koet Manufacturing Company, located in Kentucky.

From left to right: Dr. Vannevar Bush, President Harry Truman, presenting James B. Conant with the Medal of Merit and Bronze Oak Leaf Cluster on May 27, 1948.

Alien, 1948 meeting with a female, Transcript/Report: T: E/L.48:
Note
Present at the meeting:

1- A one star General
2- A Lt. Colonel
3- A languages' expert
4- Four scientists
5- Two physicians (Pathologist, and neurologist)
6- A cameraman
7- An assistant cameraman
8- A typist
9- A military personnel in charge of recording the meeting
10- Three agents from various intelligence agencies
11- An unidentified observer (A strange looking man)
12- A very important code breaker from England
13- A psychologist
14- A prominent linguist from Washington, DC
15- A university professor from Berkeley
16- Three agents from intelligence agencies (They never missed one single meeting)
17- A military man operating a speaking/communication device
18- A military man operating a recording device
19- A second cameraman
20- A second cameraman's assistant
21- A military technician handling projectors
22- A military RN (She was present at two meetings. Never to be seen again)
23- A highly decorated military pilot
24- A civilian scientist expert in mineralogy
(He was removed later)
25- Two unidentified persons. (They never said a word)
26- An unidentified person, possibly from India or Burma I am not sure. He attended two meetings.
27- Two MPs inside the room (All the time)
Outside the room:
You could see 4 MPs outside the room, nearby the door, and two additional MPs in the corridor.

*** *** ***

Q&A: Interviewing the alien.

Q: What's your name?
A: Riyah. We do not call each other (by name) unless it is very necessary because where we live the atmospheric condition does not always allow sounds to be heard. Part of our environment does not have atmosphere. And where there is no atmosphere there are two things that do not exist: Sound and Air.

Q: So how do you breath?
A: We don't need oxygen to breath. We generate our own energy to survive from our inner organism.
Energy is the most important thing in the universe.

Q: Are you built the same as us?
A: We don't have your lungs. We don't have your abdomen. So we don't eat. We don't have a digestive system.
So we don't produce wastes. We don't feel pain because we don't have a nervous system. And, we don't sense fear, simply because emotions are not wired to our cellular motor.

Q: If you don't have emotions, how do you express yourselves?
A: Humans need emotions to express themselves physically. If a person does not show emotion physically, your people, meaning humans, think he has no emotions, correct? In our case, we do not show emotions not because we don't have emotions but because we are not physicals- meaning our emotions are not physical they are mental. So this makes a big difference between us and you. You are physical and we are non physical. You live in a physical world, we live in time world.

Q: What does that mean?
A: You are limited because physical things are limited on earth.

Q: Our brain operates our physical body, how do you operate your body?

A: What you see is a frame.
I can leave it hear for you and go somewhere else.
It will disintegrate on its own and I continue somewhere else. And,
I can keep doing this endlessly.

Q: So when you want to return, do you pick up with the same
body?
A: If it's not harmed. If it disintegrates before you're eyes, then I
start with another copy of my body.

Q: But is it always the same, do you look the same?
A: Yes, and you will not notice the difference. The body you are
now looking at could be one of my copies. How would you know?

Q: So your body or whatever you call it disintegrates because the
molecules will deteriorate?
A: It disintegrates only when it is harmed.
But, our essence survives and continues somewhere else.
The essence does not disintegrate.

Q: So it lives in other dimensions?
A: Yes

Q: Can you tell us about where you're from and your dimension?
A: The name is not important because you will not find it on your
map. And the place is so far away that your mind can't understand
what it's made from.

Q: Would it be considered the 4th or 5th dimension?
A: Within each dimension beyond the physical world there are
dimensions created by each one of us.

Q: Did you mean you can create universes from the power of your
mind that you can then appear in...and you make things appear
and disappear at will?
A: We are very powerful, extremely advanced and we have seen
different and many aspects of universes that exist or will exist in
what you call the future.

There is a frontier when you cross it, you will see a great number of dimensions each one entering and exiting the other.
The essence (the alien meant what we call, the human body or human life) also can enter and exit several dimensions instantly and simultaneously.

Q: So you're saying that we can live multi-dimensionally?
A: Essences, (which mean Aliens living on different dimensions) are multi-dimensional and vibrational essences.
They can be both, physical and mental.

Q: Can you explain this?
A: You will not understand.

Q: Does one copy of yourself mirror or react to another?
And, does one have a direct impact on the other? Please explain?
A: We continue to exist through multiplication of ourselves.

Q: If your entire community is living multi-dimensionally then how?
A: Everything you have on earth we have it and nothing of what we have, you have on earth.

Q: Why is that?
A: Because we can live in a physical world and in a purely mental world. Humans can only live in a physical world.

Q: So what we need and what you need is very different.
A: We have everything we need.

Q: Is there any lack where you are from?
Here we have people that lack proper food, health care...etc.... Is there a lack of anything where you are from?
A: Only a few thousand creatures live on different planets that have needs similar to yours such as air, oxygen and food. And there are billions and billions of Essence they do not need what you need, like water, air and food because they're Essence is not made from flesh and bones that need nutrition constantly.

It is like a perfect machine which has a conscious, fairness and extremely developed intelligence.

Q: Then inside your body, you don't have blood or fluids?
A: Since we do not have circulatory system, blood circulation, we don't need the organ you call heart.
And since our essence does not have tissues and muscles, no nutrition is necessary, no food is required, no water is required to keep them functioning and growing.
We are an intelligent mechanism, very peaceful, very alert, very knowledgeable of the universe and also very familiar with you and your origin.

Q: Can you explain our origin?
A: Some of you were made from cosmic fibers you call it dust (cosmic dust).
Others were the product of what you call photosynthesis or biosynthesis.
And the rest were genetically reproduced and updated by a highly advanced race, not from Earth. And your origin is more animal than human. And at the beginning of your time on earth, some of your species, looked like reptilians, frogs, birds and other aquatic creatures. Some of your early human species, walked on three legs, others on four. And you could not tell the difference from one specie and another because all belong to the early form of the animalistic world or animals' world.

Q: So you are telling us we are animals?
A: The answer is already in your question.

Q: You don't have a circulatory system, so do you have an electrical system or how do you operate?
A: You will not understand, even if you enter the frame I have.
(The alien is referring to the physical body she used while appearing on earth).
What you will see will be very confusing to you. We are pure. We don't have waste in our bodies. We do not smell. We do not bleed. We do not feel pain. We do not feel cold. We do not feel the heat.

All of those are a sign of weakness and imperfection that you, the human being, will suffer from forever. The differences between you and us are enormous.

We are both machines. You are a destructive and self destructive machine. We are peaceful, powerful and very intelligent machine. Your brain is weak. It is not yet fully operational.

We begin to exist with a fully operationally cellular motor which has all the knowledge and information each one of us needs. Your body as a machine is made from skin, flesh, bones, and nerves.

Our essence has nothing of that.

This is why we can last for hundreds of thousands of years.

Q: So you never get sick? Do you have or need doctors?
A: Our kind does not go to what you call doctors because the body we have is reconditioned. The body (Frame) in any of its forms self adjusts, rewinds itself and starts a new.

Q: What do you mean your kind? There are other kinds?
A: Yes there are on some planets and on your own.

Q: Who are the others on earth and why are they here?
A: They were here before you. The more appropriate question would be, why are you here?

Q: So if you are not physical as you say, so why do you fly those machines, they look very physical to me?
A: Those are not flying machines, they are time-machines.

Q: You must have used a hangar or something to build those spacccrafts.
 A: Yes we did.

Our people enjoy both the physical and non physical dimensions. And, we have scientists and technicians like you do.

We do not build our vehicle gradually, as you do, in a factory.

We just produce them, ready-made.

It is similar to the process of birth in our communities, and what you call in your language, children, sons and daughters.

Q: Are you telling us you also manufacture people?
A: Our essence (creatures) are given life instantly and they are complete when they are born (Produced).
On earth a baby is born and he has to crawl and grow up. Here your children and you come to life from the womb of a female human and you grow day by day, year by year.
Our children don't have to wait that long to be fully developed. They come into existence fully grown.

Q: You mean, you give birth to a child that is a fully grown man or woman? But how old is the child, 20, 30, 40?
A: I told you before, your mind can't understand our way of life. And, how many things are created in the universe, outside your planet. In many dimensions, time does not exist therefore it's not necessary for a new born essence (creature) to wait for many years to grow up to be an adult or mature person.
There is no time. You need time to grow up. And for every year you give a number. Correct?
And you say, this person is 20 years old or 50 years old.
On our planet, we don't have age reference because no one grows older than others. You stay the same forever.
Your creator thousands of years ago created fully grown humans, man and woman, but did not survive. They died because they were not a perfect human machine. They were born with weak muscles, dysfunctional respiratory system, lack of muscular coordination and without an intelligence cellular motor.

Q: You keep talking about our creator, who are you talking about?
A: Your religious God had nothing to do with it. Some of your species, and physical forms were created and upgraded from already existing species by the Anunnaki.

Q: Are you friends with the Anunnaki, where are they now? And, do you know where they live?
A: When we enter there galaxy we see only friendship. They are not totally similar to our essence because they are corporally physical and non physical. We are physical and non physical essence. They live on Ashtari Constellation.

48

Q: What can you tell us about those small strange alien creatures that have human features and are very short. Are they like the essence, like you or other species?
A: They are from your earth and somewhere else.

Q: Where is that somewhere else?
A: It is behind your comprehension. They live on different planets, not far from each other in a zone called Naftari.

Q: Then you said, since there is no sound in other planets; therefore, no language is spoken and no words are heard, then why do you need to name this plant Naftari which has sound to it? If you have no sound then why do you have to call them by names if you can't hear them? I would not call my son George if he could not hear me because he would not respond.
A: You make too much noise on your planet. This is why you can't hear and understand each other clearly. On our planet, sounds are not heard but perceived.

Q: Can you read minds?
A: This is how partially we communicate with each other.

Q: So you live in a mute deaf world. I find this very boring.
Don't you like to hear beautiful poetry, a symphony, the rainfall, the waves or the sound of the rivers- all the beautiful sounds our nature produces?
A: We have all those, in colors and images, of such beauty and expressions that you have never seen on earth- beyond your imagination.

NOTE #1: This alien was neither an Anunnaki nor a Grey or an extraterrestrial from Zeta Reticuli. The alien belongs to the constellation of Naftari which is 150 light years from Earth.
NOTE #2: Riyah mentioned, I tried to use the simplest words possible taken from your vocabulary as transmitted through the devise I gave you.

And, you still seem unable to understand. Imagine if I had used what you call technological words and terms, then you would be completely lost.

Q: When we spoke last time you mentioned something about splitting time?
What does that mean and how does it work?
Can you please tell us what it means to stand at a place and split time?
A: You will not be able to understand but I will do my best to explain it to you briefly. It is like if you stand in front of a stage, with curtains in front.
In some of your movies theatres the first layer of curtains goes up and the second layers moves to the sides seconds later...one after another like the old musicals- very elaborate.
So, what you are seeing are two motions, simultaneously, in different dimension but occurring on the same time.

NOTE #3: The alien female looked at the General and read his thoughts right away and said, I told you, you would not understand. Let me give you an easier example.

She continued: Now you are standing in front of two large stage theatre curtains. In fact, you see one closed curtain joined together; you don't know there are two in front of you. The right side is in black, the left side is in white.
When you look first you may think this is the same curtain with two colors. However, the person that designed the curtain knows there are two pieces joined together without being sewed together by a seam.
The seamstress had just put her hand between the opening, because she knows there are two pieces and she can go through. But the others that did not make the curtains wouldn't attempt to go through it because they believe it is one piece, with two different colors.
The act or knowing that there are two pieces joined together, yet they are not.

And the fact that you can find out at distance without touching it and the fact that you go through it right away, without bumping into the whole curtain, entering into the zone behind the curtain, we call it entering a split time zone.

Now, once you are behind the curtain and it was ordered that the two curtains will be lifted up, there is nothing separating you from the point of origin, there are no more curtains. They are worthless because they do not offer a purpose, whether or not they are here, they would not prevent you from going through but apparently it stopped you from going through as a human being. This is caused by a visual understanding as explained to you by your mind. Your mind is very limited.

Q: How come you know so much about our life, custom and history and what we do on earth?
A: This is a very simple matter. Everything you do and you've done does not vanish. The substance of everything you have done, whether physical or mental takes on a new shape, a new form. Nothing in the Universe comes to an end but it transforms itself into something else. If not, the Universe will seize to exist.

If each time, part of the Universe, part of earth, part of the stars, part of the rocks, part of the air, part of the water vanishes and disappears, the Universe will be missing a lot of things. And, if this continues endlessly the Universe will be empty.

But the idea of emptiness does not exist.

There is no such thing as an empty space because if there is something like an empty space you will not be able to find it.

And, to know where this empty space is, you have to know the limit of the empty space by comparing it to a full space.

The fact that you are doing this means, you have given a size, shape, space and border to the empty space. And, when you are able to localize and define its perimeter and limits, you just proved it exists.

This is a matter of mathematics and physics, according to your science. So everything you have done on earth has been preserved from the beginning of earth time. We can tap into it, if we are interested. But we are not interested in humanity affairs. You have been broadcasting for sometime now.

51

And the frequencies of your programs and your music are well preserved. But not as many of your thought that they have reached us because we are very far away.

And all the frequencies of your noise, and music, were retained in your earth/ solar system perimeter. We knew about you, and also other advanced societies in the Universe, knew about you from a very, very long time ago. But, you had nothing to offer us. And if you wonder why then we are here on earth, if we are not interested in you I can give you lots of answers.

Some of the Galactic community members lived on earth before and your ancestors called them gods and goddesses.

Many left earth while others remained here. And with those who have remained here on earth we share information with by means and ways incomprehensive to your mind.

We enter and exit your sky/atmosphere through time pockets.

And this also is something new to you, that you now are not capable of understanding, but in the future you will.

Q: How do you explain the crash of those alien space ships? Should they crash against something physical?
A: They never crashed, they were smashed because they bumped against the time-wall.

Q: What do you mean?
A: I used the word wall so you can understand it physically. It is not a wall in the physical sense, it is a point of an entrance and exit that opens up and closes up in a matter of seconds.

When the space craft enters this point successfully, it will exit successfully. It has only a few seconds, sometimes a fraction of a second to do that. If the space craft misses the opening of the point or reaches the point that just closed it becomes solid. And, when it hits it, it smashes itself.

Q: So what we heard from other alien species about how their space craft crashed is not correct. We were told they were hit by an electrical discharge in the air that stroke their space craft, and they crashed to the ground.

A: This is not correct at all, because our communities are very advanced, even you in your limited/primitive standards, you have developed tools and ways to protect yourselves from electrical discharges and lightning.

You use a rod on the top of your buildings and homes to protect your homes from lightening and other atmospheric discharges. Many of your primitive airplanes were struck by lightning and still did not go down.

Our machines are well protected against your atmosphere elements as well as other spaces and zooming dimensions.

Q: What do you mean by zooming dimension?
A: Our machines zoom into time-space zone. Our machines don't fly like regular airplanes. They jump from one time space pocket to another time space pocket, in a non linear way.

Q: What do you mean non-linear way, is there another way to travel outside the line, you must have a track?
How will a train leave one station and arrive at the other without a track or line, if it is out of the line?
Or if it is moving in a non-linear way?
A: The way you see things on earth, the way you understand the universe, the way you set up appointments and meetings on earth is regulated and determined by time. Even your distances from one city to the next are calculated by time. Sometimes you forget about the distances between two cities or destinations, but you will know how long it will take you to get there. And, you keep looking at your watch.

This is a linear observation because you put time on one line. It is like if you take the time and put it at the border of one town and you will tell the time, drive with me, on the road to reach the other town.

So what you have done with time is make it linear. In our world, we do not travel like that. We don't make a straight line. It is a most primitive way of transportation, communication and travel since the Universe was created.

So, how do we reach our destination?
We do that by superposing it with the point of departure.

Q: This is impossible. None of our scientists agree with this.
A: We already know that, and this is why you are unable to reach us, luckily.

Q: So tell me now, if we fly your machine, you're saying, we're able to enter this non-linear rendezvous point and exit somewhere else? Is that correct?
A: No.

Q: Why not, we are flying the same machine?
A: That's the problem with you understanding the whole concept. First, our machines don't fly, they jump, and they zoom in and zoom out.
Second, they are not controlled by a dashboard or a navigation system, or with anything on your regular airplane.
They are controlled by our mind. We are part of our machines and our machines are an extension of our mental energy. So, you will not know how to operate those machines. And I know you have already inspected the interior of some of those machines and you could not find what you were looking for.
There are no gears, to take off or to land, no steering wheel and no navigation system. What you saw was only a screen. And, a head band attached to the pilot of the machine.
So this band received the order from our cell and transmits it to the machine. And this band works only on our cellular motor (means the alien brain; they call it cellular motor), which contains trillion upon trillions of cells, almost all are functional.

NOTE #4: Here, for the first time, the military, the scientists and others, who were present at the meeting, remained silent for 20 seconds. This had never happened before.
And, they were staring at each other. The alien apparently was addressing herself particularly to the general by moving the contour of her body toward the general.
The alien continued: Go ahead and call them, it's ok. Ask them to send you the band to look at it.

NOTE #5: I found this fascinating because the female alien already read the thought and intention of the general, who in fact, was going to call The Pentagon to ask them to send the band to him so their scientists could view and study it from this new point of view offered by the alien.
He was hoping to find out how this band could be used as a communication and navigation tool.

NOTE #6: Following this line of questions there was other information that was shared in the meeting; however, I am not at liberty to share the details because they are of a military nature rotating around weapon systems, strategies and national security.
So, we will move on to other discussions with different alien species that occurred at different times with other teams, including the military and scientists.

*** *** ***

Comments:

Throughout the entire meeting, the alien was not communicating verbally; no sound was heard from her.
Her communication was directly transmitted from her brain (cellular motor) to the device she gave us.
The device will receive her thought and answer in colors, images and frequencies, like we use to send messages through the Morse code.
At the far end of the machine, there is a screen which displays dots, multiple dots, empty spaces, and slashes and deciphers the letters or forms.
Secondly, after this was displayed on the screen, the machine would talk to us, in English, in a very and most un-usual English vocabulary. For example, the alien never used pronouns, such as "I" and occasionally she would use "we".
The alien never said we have a body; instead she said, we have an Essence. It took the military quite a while to re-interpret her English into their English. And, quit often they missed the point.

A major part of her mind transmission was lost in the translation. Later on the military decided firmly that top notch linguists in the country should be present at all meetings with aliens.
Hopefully to help translate and interpret the alien languages and expressions correctly.
Weeks later, I discovered that this was absolutely true because the alien device contained a limited amount of English vocabulary.
And, the words used mentally by the alien, technologically transmitted and displayed by the machine were those often used by the military in their daily life- normal everyday slang.
It was very obvious, to me, that all her answers were not given to us with technological and scientific terms. At one point the female alien told us she avoided that on purpose.

Note: An insider (A foreign scientist, naturalized American) who attended the meeting said verbatim, "And, should she had decided to answer us in alien technology, her language and scientific terms...we would not have understood anything because those alien scientific and technology terms could not be found in our dictionary and science books.
So, she did her best to use common words known to the majority of people on earth."

Worth mentioning here, the alien described the time-space exit and entrance as pockets while the military called it rendezvous.
The military inquired about navigation system of the alien craft. The alien used the term mental command.
There is no navigation.
The military used the expression "flying machines."
The alien used jumping machine. The military used the word or terms linear distance, linear time- to get from one place to another. The alien said that non-linear is a juxtaposition of two destinations. Consequently, everything we believed in, including what the military and the scientists at the meeting believed in, was in sharp contract, opposition and contradiction with what the alien meant and explained.

At one point, it was decided by some scientists, that the amount of earth vocabulary should be increased and pictures be added to the device to widen the spectrum of receiving messages and interpreting them.

Regarding this, the aliens told them they did not need to do this because in the next meeting with other visitors, they will be able to communicate with them in mechanical English.

The general picked up the phone and talked to someone, we were not sure who. And then, one or two minutes later, a captain entered the room and whispered something in the ear of the general.

The general then said, "Ok folks, that's it for today. Let's wrap it up. Only military personal stand by, others, we'll see you later".

Following the general's orders asking the civilians to leave, two of the team of scientists were glad to leave the meeting so they could share and have a discussion about what just took place. As the two scientists walked down the long corridor they were followed by two MPs (Military Police).

One scientist commented how refreshing that the MPs were not carrying guns. He said "Wow, they must be getting civilized".

The other scientist, who was a noted scientist in Nazi Germany, then commented, word-for-word, "Why the military would not allow us to come to any of the first meetings with any of the aliens and why we were not allowed to know where or what galaxy they came from?"

As they kept walking in the corridor a few seconds later, a captain came outside and followed the group of scientist asking one of them, Dr. Teller (who later became the father of the American Hydrogen Bomb), "Please go back to the room" (Dr. Teller was the only one who was allowed to stay in the room!)

The other scientists were bewildered and wondered why he was the only scientist to be asked back to the room. They wondered, was this some sort of favoritism?

Many of the scientists were pissed off as they were leaving the base.

Dr. Hermann Oberth

The foremost authority on rocketry outside the United States was Dr. Hermann Oberth, a Hungarian-born German. In 1923, he published a book about rocket travel into outer space. Because of his important writings, many small rocket societies sprang up around the world. In the spring of 1930, a young Wernher von Braun assisted Oberth in his early experiments in testing a liquid-fueled rocket with about 15 pounds of thrust. Photo & text credit: NASA.

Dr. Hermann Oberth had access to the "Aliens Transcripts".He stated: "We cannot take credit for our record advancement in certain scientific fields alone; we have been helped "people of other worlds."

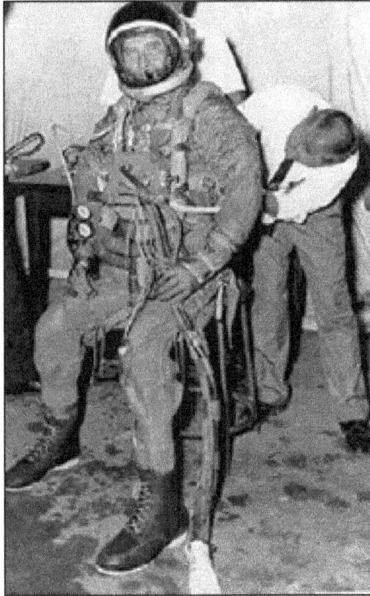

Dr. von Braun

Dr. von Braun suiting up prior to entering Marshall's neutral buoyancy tank. Credit NASA. Dr. von Braun admitted on more than one occasion that he got help from the extraterrestrials. He was directly involved in the recovery of a crashed alien spacecraft (UFO; crescent shape) and alien reverse engineering from 1947 to 1949.

Dr. Von Braun, right, holds the coveted Hermann Oberth award, presented to him by Dr. Oberth, left, on October 19, 1961, during an Alabama Section Meeting of the American Rocket Society. Early in his career, Von Braun was a student of Oberth, one of the world's foremost theorists on space propulsion. Source/Credit: NASA.

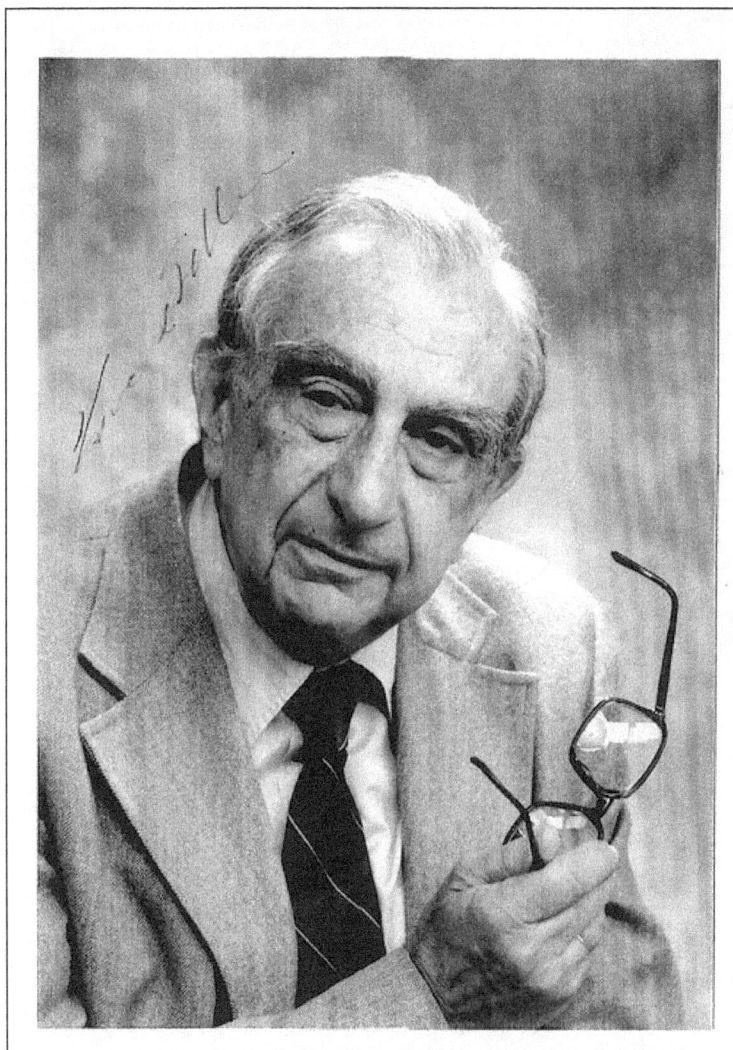

Dr. Ed Teller.

Dr. Teller submitted a detailed report on UFO and alien reverse engineering to Presidents Truman and Reagan.

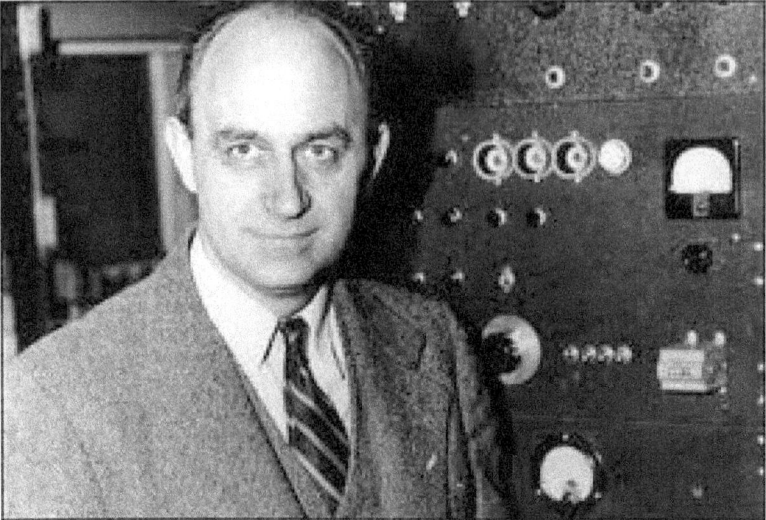

Dr. Enrico Fermi.
One of the architects of the pre-Philadelphia Experiment, and prime reviewer of the Aliens Transcripts.

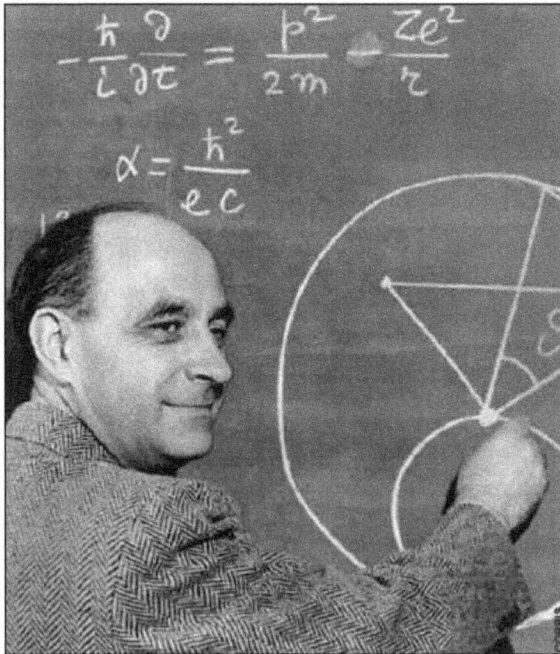

$$-\frac{\hbar}{i}\frac{\partial}{\partial t} = \frac{p^2}{2m} - \frac{Ze^2}{r}$$

$$\alpha = \frac{\hbar^2}{ec}$$

Dr. Enrico Fermi

Ironically, at the same time, an old Plymouth or a Dodge, with a military tag/license plate parked outside, and Dr. von Braun (the Father of the American Space Program who put us on the moon) was seen getting out of the car.

It became very apparent to me that the military did not trust all the scientists and vice-versa.

The scientists the military felt comfortable working with were:

1-Dr. Herman Oberth
2-Dr. von Braun
3-Dr. Edward Teller
4-Dr. Enrico Fermi.

*** *** ***

Explanation of the alien's answers:

The aliens' answer: *"We do not call each other by name unless it is very necessary because where we live the atmospheric condition does not always allow sounds to be heard. Part of our environment does not have atmosphere. And where there is no atmosphere there are two things that do not exist: Sound and Air."*

"We do not call each other".

The device used to communicate with the alien did not contain enough words from our vocabulary (English language), to correctly, adequately and completely record and transmit what the alien really meant.

The device contained very limited number of words. For example "Call" meant communicate, and not talking to somebody or emitting a vocal sound.

The alien meant by "Call" a straightforward communication using mental frequency.

Of course, aliens are capable of producing sounds and vocal expressions. But their most common way of communicating with each other is via mental images' projections that take real form in their "Cellular Motor" (Brain' cells).

Yes, they are capable of producing and hearing voices, noises and sounds.

From left to right: Inventor, Freddie Williams and Tom Kilburn
at the central control panel of the Manchester's first Baby
computer, in England, 1948.

The first type of "Communication Device":
The first type of "Communication Device" used in the early
meetings was called CTF (Transmission Channel); originally
"Channel of the transmission frequency of aliens." By the mid of
November or December of 1948, the name was changed to TD
(Talking Device).

In the early draft of "Contact", a science-fiction novel by Dr. Carl Sagan, the alien's device was mentioned. But as expected, it was deleted in the final copy of the book, just a few days before it was submitted to the publisher. I do not blame Dr. Sagan; I am sure he had some serious reasons for deleting any reference made to the alien's communication device.
"unless it is very necessary."
The alien meant, unless it is instant.
The word *necessary* was a wrong interpretation.
And "instant" meant, at the time aliens' brains (Cellular Motors) are tuned to different communication frequencies.

In another meeting, the alien did briefly explain how the cells in their brain (Cellular Motors) function; she said that their brains contains billions upon billions of cells interconnected to a main mental center of energy and collectively wired to other aliens' brains. Thus, mental communications are instant.

Their "Cellular Motor" is not made from flesh and blood, but rather from channels and depots of knowledge and information data-base. She also said, while communicating with others, she can easily and instantly communicate with different groups using different emission channels. It is like listening to a radio set capable of simultaneously transmitting different radio shows, programs and talks, and listening to all of them by turning the knob to one specific station.
I know it is not so easy to comprehend how this could be done.
None of our scientists could figure it out. Our team of scientists was puzzled by this, and decided to contact Freddie William and his team in England to find out how multiple transmissions (Radio or other medium) can be sent simultanously to one station, aired by the same station without "parasite", and clearly received/heard by listners. Worth mentioning here that the team of William were the inventors of of the RASD (Random Access Storage Device For Computer), in 1948.
Bell Laboratories were also contacted by our scientists and the military, because at that time, Bell scientists were woking on the first "TR" (Transistor Radio)

The aliens (Intraterrestrials and other species) upgraded our 1947-1951 technology to an unimaginable level.

First laser transmission hologram, by Emmett Leith and Juris Upatnieks, in 1964, but originally conceived and developed in 1948 by Dennis Gabor (The 1971 Nobel Prize Winner), who was one of the leading scientific advisors to the military, and who has elaborately commented on the Aliens' Transcripts.

Two of these discoveries (Upgraged/enhanced technology) were:
a- The cellular communications. Based upon technology given to us by the aliens, Bell Laboratories developed the first mobile telephone.
b-The prototype of the transistor, created in late 1947, and perfected to a certain degree in 1948 by Bell labs. The aliens did not get any credit, instead, three scientists from Bell Laboratories received the Nobel Prize for their scientific discovery!

*** *** ***

Photo: Inventor Dennis Gabor.
Born in Budapest, Hungary, on June 5, 1900, and died on February 8, 1979.
He was a major scientific link between the aliens and Earth's technology.
In 1972, he admitted that he had much unfinished technological work on his hands, and part of it was closely related to alien reverse-engineering.

Worth mentioning here that another major scientific breakthrough came in the form of "Laser", also developed by Bell, and based upon aliens' technology. Bell was (and still is) one of the first, principal and major military contractors.

Just read between the lines, what Arthur L. Schawkow, the 1981 Nobel Prize Winner for Laser Spectroscopy, wrote: "When the first lasers were operated, I and other scientists close to the research were surprised at how easy it turned out to be.

We had assumed that, since lasers had never been made, it must be very difficult. But once you knew how, it was not at all difficult. Mostly what had been lacking were ideas and concepts."

"because where we live the atmospheric condition does not always allow sounds to be heard."

The alien meant, that atmospheric conditions change from one space zone to another space zone. In other words, in entering different dimensions or other galaxies, aliens can hear sounds that usually are not "registered" on their main planet.

"Part of our environment does not have atmosphere."

The alien meant that a specific zone in the atmosphere of her planet does not have "Earth's atmosphere." This does not mean that their entire planet is without an atmosphere.

In another meeting, she did explain to us, that within one dimension of her planet, there are multiple layers of inner layers of different dimensions. It is like the old fashion way of typing on a typewriter and making carbon copies.

You type once, but what you typed is instantly copied on other copies. It is one stack of papers, but each one has a different zone, a different atmosphere, and is totally separated from the other carbon-copies, yet, all copies remain an integral part of what you have typed. This is another confusing explanation for how a single planet can have multiple and different atmospheres.

"We do not need oxygen to breath. We generate our own energy to survive from our inner organism.
Energy is the most important thing in the universe."

Note: Our scientists were debating this issue.

Each one had a personal opinion (Theory) about the kind of energy, the alien was talking about.

Some believed it was some sort of bio-organic energy. The alien said NO! Others assumed that it was some sort of cellular-electric energy. And the alien said, "You are getting closer."

And she added, "Electricity as you know it is a very primitive kind of energy."

Some thought that the alien is a "Programmed Intelligence responding to electric pulses created by structural channels inside her body."

Worth mentioning here that Isaac Asimov was called in to give his opinion, and it was during a session he had with the military, that he came up with the word "Robotic" (First time ever used) referring to the mechanism and functioning of the body of the alien. And the rest is history.

Years later, an avalanche of scientists, as well as science-fiction writers will adopt that term and incorporate it in their papers and writings.

One of the most distinguished one was Norbert Wiener (1894-1964) who has developed the notion and principles of cybernetics.

*** *** ***

68

Norbert Wiener

Isaac Asimov coined the terms "Robots", and "Robotics". And very few know why and how he came up with these two terms. But scientists and military men who were involved in dealing with aliens know very well, when, how and why, Asimov came up with these terms.

69

Comments on an early meeting with "Riyah", a female alien.

The alien communicated with us through her "Cellular Motor".

Throughout the entire meeting, the alien was not communicating verbally; no sound was heard from her. Her communication was directly transmitted from her brain (cellular motor) to the device she gave us.

The device would receive her thoughts and answer in colors, images and frequencies. At the far end of the machine, a screen displayed dots, multiple dots, empty spaces, and slashes and deciphered letters and symbols.

After the alien's message was displayed on the screen, the machine would talk to us in English, in a very and most unusual English vocabulary. For example, the alien never used pronouns, such as "I" and occasionally she would use "we".

Her sentences were short. Her statements were very scientific, precise, and mind-bending.

The alien never said we have a body; instead she said, "we have an Essence."

"We did not fully understand the alien's language."

It took the military quite a while to re-interpret and translate her alien English into ours.

And quite often they missed the point. A major part of her mind transmission was lost in the translation. Later on, the military decided that top notch linguists should be present at all meetings with aliens, so they would or could translate and interpret the alien's language and expressions correctly, and in their entirety.

"Two or three days later, I discovered that this was absolutely true because the alien device contained a limited amount of English vocabulary..." said a leading cryptologist/linguist. "And the words mentally used by the female alien, technologically transmitted and displayed by the machine were those often used by the military in a slang manner..." commented another linguist.

It was very obvious to me, that all her answers were not given to us in scientific terms we could understand.

At one point she told us that she avoided that on purpose.

And should she had decided to answer us in alien technology's terminology/vocabulary, her language and scientific terms would leave us with more confusion, because aliens' terms could not be found in our dictionaries and science books. So, she did her best to use "common words and terms known to the majority of the people" who were present during the meeting. At one point, it was decided by some scientists, that the amount of "Earth vocabulary" should be increased and pictures be added to the device to widen the spectrum of messages' reception and interpretation.

The aliens told them they did not need to do this because in the next meeting with other visitors, they will be able to communicate with them in "mechanical English."

The meetings' dates:

The meetings were spread over a period of 4 days:

Date of the first meeting: Monday, 2, February 1948. 9:00 AM.

Date of the second meeting: Tuesday 3, February 1948. 9:00 AM.

Date of the third meeting: Thursday 5, February 1948. 9:00 AM.

Date of the fourth meeting: Saturday 7, February 1948. 9:00 AM.

From a meeting's transcripts during the late period of 1948:

Topics discussed:

1- Alien spacecrafts diving into the ocean.

2- Origin of alien spacecrafts.

3- Who is piloting aliens' spacecrafts?

4- Purposes.

5- How do they move/operate underwater?

6- Their mode of operation and source of energy.

7- Non-human species living on planet Earth.

8- Mitra: Cold Plasma

Present at the meeting:

1-Two star General...

2- Lt. Colonel...

3- Dr. Edward Teller

4- Dr. ...

5- Dr. ...

6- Major...

7- A very important code breaker from England
8- A psychologist
9- A neurologist
10- A prominent linguist
11- A university professor from Berkeley
12- Three agents from intelligence agencies
13- A military man operating a speaking/communication device
14- A military man operating a recording device
15- A cameraman
16- A cameraman's assistant
17- A military technician handling projectors
18- A military RN
19- A highly decorated military pilot
20- A civilian scientist expert in mineralogy.
He was removed later.
21- Two unidentified persons
22- An unidentified person, possibly from India or Burma.(I am not sure)
23- Two MPs inside the room.
Outside the room:
You could see 4 MPs outside the room, nearby the door, and two additional MPs in the corridor.

Q&A: Interviewing the alien.
A Colonel asked the alien if any of their spacecrafts has entered our oceans. The alien answered no.
The Colonel seemed to be confused.
Perhaps, he did not believe the alien, because he commented on the alien's answer by saying, "We have seen them...."
Aliens: Not ours.

Question: Not yours? Meaning what?
Alien: We have no need to enter your oceans.

Question: Apparently some did.
We saw something diving into the ocean. They were not ours.
How do you explain this?
What do you have to say about this?

Alien: They belong to another race.

Question: Wow!! Who? What race?
Another alien race? How many are they?
From outer space?
Alien: Not from outer space.

Question: Where from then? The moon? Mars?
Alien: For your planet.

Question: Oh no!!! Not from here, I bet on it.
Answer: Your knowledge is very limited.

Question: Then tell me about it.
Alien: They are from your planet. They belong to a galactic race living on your planet. They are not from our world.

Note: This wasn't...much...of...help...replied the Lt. Colonel. (Unreadable words.)
I could not clearly read the question/response of the military man in its entirety. A few lines were missing, and the ink was smeared on the page.
But you got the meaning. The military man was not satisfied by the alien's answer, because she did not give him the specific origin of those spacecrafts, and did not elaborate enough on the identity of their pilots.
A few months later, it became clear to us, that those alien spacecrafts were made by and piloted by an alien race that has lived here on Earth for millions of years, and long before modern Man walked on the surface of the globe.
The aliens have huge habitats underwater as well as on remote areas inaccessible to us.
Some 70 or 75 years ago, we organized and funded an expedition to those remote areas, and two additional expeditions to the North Pole. And what we found was beyond belief and absolutely mind-bending.

Some initial reports confirmed the existence of "Bizarre locations and compounds" and contained self-explanatory notes such as:
1-"Unknown to us",
2-"Not Man-made",
3-"Extensive structures made from materials unknown to us",
4-"Defies explanation..."

Dr. Teller asked the alien about the propulsion system of those alien crafts, and how they operate underwater.
The alien replied (As she did many times before) that he will not be able to understand, mainly because our science books and scientific research do not have the aliens' technological and scientific terms, and corresponding information, explanation and description.
Secondly, because the propulsion technology used by the aliens contradict our laws of physics.
Dr. Teller was persistent and replied, "Let me be the judge of that..."
Another scientist asked whether there is any sort of combustion, an anti-gravity propeller, electro-magnetic channel or current, an aquatic source of energy, etc. And the alien replied NO!
The alien added that once the spacecraft enters the water, it takes on different scientific properties; the craft does not plunge in the water as we have assumed. It does not dive.
In fact, it never touches the surface of the water.
In some incomprehensible manner, the craft creates some sort of vacuum tunnel before it penetrates the water.
Inquiring about the "Vacuum Tunnel", a scientist asked whether the tunnel can be measured, whether the tunnel is made from materials found on Earth, or whether the tunnel is created by the spacecraft itself, and could this tunnel be detected by us.
The alien answered that the tunnel could NOT be detected by us, nor measured, because it is movable, temporarily used, it is not physical, and could not be detected by any sonar system.

Dr. Teller asked the alien about the "invisible" structure of the aliens' tunnel and what it consists of. The alien said, it is "Mitra" (Cold Plasma.)
I am absolutely sure that back then in mid 1948, none of our scientists understood or fully comprehended what a Cold Plasma was?!
In 2010, I tried very modestly to explain this tunnel on the History Channel. The best way I could have described it is by calling it "Corridor Plasma"; a term mentioned by the Grays.

None of our contemporary scientists, Americans and foreigners, military or civilians commented on what I have said, for obvious reasons: Firstly, they don't know, nor do I! And secondly, many of them reject the whole idea, while a few sincere scientists are still inquiring about this fantastic technology and intensifying their research in the field of aquatic cold plasma.
Today, in 2014, I have a different opinion about all this; our military scientists know exactly and very well what an "Aquatic Cold Plasma" is. And I am delighted to learn that.
This technology is needed on so many levels, especially in the field of global energy, solar energy, cosmic energy, Earth energy and domestic energy we use on a daily basis.
AUTEC has become the front leader in this area. And without any hesitation or restriction I would say Mazel Tov!

From a transcript of a meeting in early 1949:
Present at the meeting:
Note: Access to the list of attendees was restricted.
Questions and Answers:
Question: Can you tell me how many different races there are on your planet?
Alien: Many.
Different Essences, structures and different categories.
Question: Do you communicate with all of them?
Alien: Yes.
Question: So, how do you communicate with all of them?
Alien: In many different ways.
We use our cellular motor.

75

We use images projected mentally.
We use graphs.
We use mind transmission channels.
We use collective transmission.

Question: Why haven't they communicated with us?
Alien: Give me one good reason why should they communicate with you. Would you communicate with inferior species?
What would you learn from them?
You don't even know how to communicate with each other. You don't know how to communicate with animals. You don't know how to communicate with nature. We find it very amusing that you have thousands of different languages on earth, instead of one which everyone could understand.
First, learn how to communicate with your own kind; and after, invite other civilizations to communicate with you.

Question: Do they know about us?
Alien: Yes. The Universe is not divided.
The Universe has no frontiers.
Your world is divided by the frontiers you created.

Question: Are they hostile?
Alien: Some. Few. Very few.

Question: What do they look like?
Alien: Some are without a Frame (physical structure).
Some purely cellular.
Some purely mental.
Some ethero-organic.
Some vibrational.
Some multi-dimensional.
Some physical.
Some physical-mental.
Some superposed presences.
Some exist between parallel dimensions.
Some are from the future.
Some did not exist yet.

Some are what we call penetrating vibrations.
Some organic.
Some spheric.
And some other "Essences" your mind cannot understand.
Some have all your physical senses and faculties but do not have ears to hear, eyes to see, mouths to taste, hands to feel because those organs are completely useless outside your world.

Question: Do they understand any of our languages?
Alien: Not all of them. No reason to.
They are not interested in your kind. But your languages can be easily understood by us once they are fed to our machines.

Question: Do they have any intentions of contacting us?
Alien: Some did in the past. There is a non human race that is in contact with you because they are concerned with earth safety, for they consider earth as their own habitat.

Question: What should we do in the event they do contact us?
Alien: It depends on the race that communicates with you or suddenly appears in your world. If they are hostile, there is nothing you can do because they are far more advanced than you. It would be a bad day for earth. It is not advisable for your kind to try to communicate with other species, for your own safety.

Note: According to the alien, it's best not to try to contact any of the other species because you cannot be sure who you may come in contact with. You may find yourself contacting a race that has hostile tendencies.
Therefore, for the safety of earth, contacting other species is not recommended. (It's like somebody knocking at your door, after midnight, in a remote area. It's a risk to open the door because you don't know who is going to be there).
This was a common practice of our American frontier pioneers in the old wild West, who always had their riffles handy, living in fear, and preparing for the unknown as a means of protection, especially against strangers and intruders.

They would immediately reach for their guns, revolvers and riffles.

Question: Do they have a planetary system similar to ours?
Alien: Yes, but on a much larger scale.
Your planet has one moon, other planets may have up to five moons. Some planets have no gravity, some planets are anti-gravity, some planets have heavier gravity than earth. So now you might understand why other races look very differently from your kind. Their anatomy and physiognomy will scare you terribly as you, might scare other races who are not highly developed.

Note: Other races are not highly developed, by the alien's standards, not by earth standards because we are still at the very bottom of cosmic civilization.
And, what the alien considered not highly advanced alien civilizations are unquestionably millions of years ahead of us.

Question: So, why are you here? What made you come?
Alien: You are on our way.

Question: What do you mean, on your way? Where?
Alien: Earth and your solar system and their location in the Milky Way are our passage to other galaxies.

Question: Have you been here before?
Alien: Yes.

Question: Have we been visited by other races from outside our solar system?
Alien: Yes.

Question: How far from Earth is the nearest civilized intelligent species?
Alien: Fifteen light years.

Question: What language do they speak?

Alien: I have already explained to you how other civilizations, including ours, communicate with each other.
However, there are sixteen civilizations whose languages are very similar to a phonetic language the Anunnaki used when they came to earth. Your early ancestors in some part of earth have learned that language. But, wars and foreign invasions of their land, erased that language.
In doing so you have lost your greatest opportunity to keep a link with far more advanced civilizations.

Note: The alien meant that when nations or groups of highly developed people loose their language because of destructive means and domination by aggressive foreign forces, Earth looses a major and essential part of its history and cultural wealth. And as a result, a major aspect of its authentic identity suffers.
So, we, humans, lost a direct link to our past and our origin.
Really, we don't know very much about our ancient history and the early history of civilization on Earth because no language was left or preserved to learn about highly developed or advanced civilizations who lived on Earth before we invented ice cream cones, and hot dogs at Coney Island.
This is unfortunately what happened to Phoenicia when it was destroyed by Alexander the Great and absorbed by the Roman Empire. As soon as the Phoenician language died out, Phoenicia and its civilization died as well.

Question: How advanced are they?
Alien: Some millions of years, others billions of years ahead of you.

Question: How old are they?
Alien: As old as the Universe itself, as old as the cosmic energy because everything is made from the cosmic energy. The Essence never dies; it is transformed and re-transformed endlessly.

Question: What do they think of us?
Alien: I have already answered this question. I sense fear in your question.

Question: Do they have a structured social system?
Alien: It is a collective awareness. From our very limited knowledge of your English language, I can freely tell you that we do not have a pronoun like the word "I"; simply because, it is considered a manifestation of egotism.

Note: The alien meant that the word/pronoun "I" is contrary to the collective consciousness or universal oneness their society lives by.

Question: How would you describe their anatomy?
Alien: I have already answered this question. Rewind the screen (she means the messages received by the speaking device).
Question: What is their average life-span?
Alien: It depends on each civilization, some are constantly superposed, multiplied and reproduced. Some live millions of years, others hundreds of thousands of years. It all depends on the level of their development, advancement, technology and cosmic awareness. And some who are an essential part of the cosmic particles never die.

Note: It is very striking to hear the alien's answer because some 60 years later, our scientist are still trying to discover at CERN, what they call the "God's particle". This is exactly what the alien referred to in 1948.

Question: Do they believe in God?
Alien: I have already answered this question. Rewind the tapes of the speaking device.
Note: The previous answer was: Each Universe has its own god.

Question: Do they have armed forces?
Alien: They have organized forces.
Those who live in lower dimensions do have aggressive means, and they are quite destructive. This is why I already advised you never to try to communicate with what or who when you don't know who that may be.

Question: How advanced are they?
Alien: You have a tendency to repeat the same questions over and over again. I have already answered this question.
Rewind the screen.
I can read your mind, you are not without intelligence.
You are testing my consistency.
This is part of your weakness. Suspicions are self-destructive.

Note: When she said that, two military men, the scientists and one anthropologist started to nod and shake their heads after her response.
Following the meeting, they noted that perhaps they should start keeping their questions more consistent since her memory is impeccable and that perhaps they should start to be totally honest with her. After all she does read minds.
One military man had another idea.
He said, don't do that yet; how about if you repeat the same question right away, back to back, over and over again perhaps she's a recording device, how do we know. (My personal belief is that his intention was to trick her.)
Outside the meeting, the same military man said to the group of scientists, do you remember what Isaac Asimov told us, she's a machine, he called her a robot. I don't know what the hell a robot is but he made it clear that this is a machine and this machine has some sort of leathery skin.
In 1948, the first time the words Robot and Robotics were coined by Isaac Asimov. It was too early for the military or non-military to fully understand what the word robot meant. Even when the word robot was used in one of the meetings with the alien, the alien herself did not understand what was meant by the word because it was not yet entered in our common vocabulary, especially in the vocabulary of our languages randomly selected by the alien.
The scientists found the military man's suggestion silly and childish to mess with an alien who is millions of years ahead of them.
They collectively decided that all questions will be agreed upon before they go inside again to meet with the alien.

This was sparked because there were two sets of questions: One from the scientists, which was approved by the top brass, and the other, from the military which the scientists never had a chance to review. The General in charge of the meeting did not agree at first because quite often during the course of the session the General would ask the civilians to leave the room, especially when dealing with questions and answers pertaining to national security, weaponry and strategies supplied by the alien.

Finally, the group decided to combine one list with both the military and scientist questions.

And collectively they finally agreed to be honest and straight forward with the alien.

Worth mentioning here that one very considerate scientist made the point that, he did not care if this "thing" (Meaning the alien) was a robot, a machine or whatever, "that this alien, regardless of what it is, has more spirituality than any of us!"

Question: How would you define a scientifically advanced civilization?

Alien: When you don't use power or aggression to convince others, you are on your way to civilization.

When you look toward the universe and other communities before you look at yourself, you are on your way to civilization. When you get rid of your weapons, any tools of destruction, you are on your way to civilization.

When you open your hand and extend your arm to welcome other realms of knowledge and wisdom rather than close your hands, make fists for war and stiffen your jaw, then you are on your way to civilization.

When you stop to have locks on your doors and fear intrusions, you are on your way to civilization.

When you unify one language for all the people of your kind, you are on your way to civilization.

When you stop to categorize people by gender, by race and by colors, you are on your way to civilization.

When you are no longer in need of law enforcements, judges, jails, courts and punishment, you are on your way to civilization.

When you get rid of your monetary system, you are on your way to civilization.

When you stop killing living creatures (animals and creatures of the sea) and eating their flesh and blood, you are on your way to civilization.

When you stop dropping your waste in the oceans and polluting your environments, you are on your way to civilization.

When you get rid of your organized religions and scare people by false threats such as burning in hell and alike, you will be on your way to civilization.

Finally, when you start to believe in the divine essence of yourself and the spiritual mental immortality of your very being, you will be on your way to civilization. But, we know you will never do any of the above.

Note: One anthropologist who was listening to the alien's answer had tears in his eyes.

You would think that the attendees at the meeting would be motivated and impressed by what she said. Absolutely not.

Instead, many of the group continued to hammer the alien with tricky questions. The alien was unable to express her disgust through facial expressions, because she was not 100% physical.

But, in someway it was very obvious how she felt about the line of questioning and our selfish intentions.

Question: How many advanced civilizations are in the universe?
Alien: Billions.

Question: Where does the universe begin and end?
Alien: The universe began before time and space was created. There is no beginning and no ending for the ever expanding and ever lasting universe.

Question: How would you explain the creation of the universe?
Alien: I have already answered this question.

Question: How would you explain time?

Alien: Time is a notion created by your kind.
You can't measure time unless you transcend it.
In your current condition, and based on your level of science and technology, you can't do that yet; and consequently, you could not understand what time is. In your mind, time is measured by space and distances that separate you. From what you are looking at, or trying to reach.
And, this is why you will never be able to understand time as long as you attach it to a distance and motion of objects.

Question: How would you explain the relation between time and space?
Alien: One contains the other. One eliminates the other.

Question: Which is bigger and more important, time or space?
Alien: What is beyond time and space.

Question: How do you measure time?
Alien: Time cannot be measured. It is your kind's perception of what it can't be measured and evaluated. Yet you live by it.

Question: How do you measure space?
Alien: We don't.

Question: Is there something in the universe faster than the speed of light?
Alien: Yes. The cellular motor's speed.

Question: How do you measure it?
Alien: We don't. It is faster than us. And since it is part of us and we are part of it, we become one with it.
You can't measure what is your Essence, because you will limit it and prevent it from growing.

Question: What is your agenda?
Alien: No agenda.

Question: Is it shared by other civilizations?

Alien: No. I just told you we have no agenda.
You are not listening!

Question: Do you consider us an advanced civilization?
Alien: No.

Question: What it would take for a civilization to be considered civilized and advanced?
Alien: I have already answered this question.

Question: Do you have any kind of surveillance or monitoring system strong enough to monitor Earth? All of it?
Alien: Yes.

Question: How does it work?
Note: The alien refused to answer.

Question: Is it from outer space or in our atmosphere?
Note: The alien refused to answer.

Question: Let me ask you this, are you willing to share with us some of your technology?
Alien: Not yet.

Question: Do you have weather on your planet?
Alien: Yes, but not necessary atmosphere.

Question: Can you control the weather?
Alien: Yes.

Question: How do you control the weather?
Note: The alien refused to answer.

Question: How can we convince your people we are a peaceful nation?
Alien: We already know your intentions. You can't.

Question: Do you have a centralized military command?

Alien: Yes.

Question: Who is in charge of your centralized military command?
Note: The alien refused to answer.

Question: Do you have a naval fleet?
Note: The alien refused to answer.

Question: Do you have military ranks? A military hierarchy?
Alien: Yes.

Question: Would you describe your military ranks and military hierarchy to us?
Note: The alien refused to answer.

Question: When you meet with other races...do you meet with them physically or mentally?
Do you use a physical body or something else?
Alien: It depends on the nature and structure of their Essence.

Question: In your part of the Universe, do you use the same crafts you use to come to Earth?
Alien: If necessary.

Question: Meaning what?
Alien: We do, if we enter a dense physical dimension. But we can always do it without machines...very easily.
If the time-space pockets do not respond, we then use ort time-machines.

Question: What is a time-machine?
Alien: A tool that does not bend or fail while entering multiple or consecutive parallel dimensions, unless it misses times-space pockets.

Question: The one you used to come to Earth...is it a time-machine?
Alien: Yes.

Question: Is Earth a consecutive parallel dimension?
Alien: Yes. Part of it.

Question: Then why did you use a time-machine and not another "tool"? Earth is a dense physical dimension? Isn't it?
Alien: Not always.

Question: What do you mean not always?
Alien: We do not enter your space.
We do not fly in your atmosphere. We zoom in.
This eliminates any density.

Note: None of the attendees understood a word. I can guarantee you that. The presiding General told the two scientists who were hammering the alien with this sort of questions to move on to another area of questioning.
He instructed them to ask more specific questions closely related to space-strategies and operational procedures of the crafts.

Question: Do you believe in God?
Alien: Which one?

Question: Our God!
Alien: Each Universe has its own god, which is the "Highest Essence". I have already answered this question so many times. You are wasting your time. And your intentions are very clear to me. No, I will not contradict myself. I am remember everything I have said in the past. Rewind the machine.

Question: Do you believe in hell?
Alien: No.

Question: Do you believe in heaven, the Christian Paradise?
Alien: No.

Question: Do you believe in the final judgment?
Alien: It happens every day.

Question: What do you mean?
Alien: It happens as you speak. You are your own final judgment.

Question: Do you believe in reincarnation?
Alien: No.

Question: How old is the Universe?
Alien: 80 trillions by your time's standard, space, and distance.
And much less by our standards. You can't understand now.

Question: Who created the Universe?
Alien: Itself.

Question: Please explain.
Alien: The Universe came to exist before time and space existed.

Question: What do you mean?
Alien: There is no beginning otherwise the Universe would need a
creator.

Question: Do you mean the Universe created itself?
Alien: Not exactly.

Question: Would you please clarify?
Alien: You would never understand unless you get outside time
and space.

Question: How canweI do that?
Alien: In your situation and condition, you can't.

Question: Can you?
Alien: Yes.

Question: How come?
Alien: Because I am not a physical entity.

Question: Meaning what?

Alien: I am not trapped or defined by age, space, or time. Possibly by memory if needed.

Question: Memory? What kind of memory?
Alien: The one that gives me a "Frame"; the one I use when I enter a physical dimension.

Question: I don't understand.
Alien: I already know that. Look at the screen (Speaking Device).

Question: Why don't we get rid of this machine and talk in plain English. Or why don't you teach us your language?
This will save us lots of trouble. It is very confusing you know. You don't understand our language and we don't understand yours.

Alien: Confusing to your kind, only.

Question: Are your people aware of your situation?
Do they know you are here?
Do they know you are talking to us?
Alien: Yes. Affirmative.

Question: How do they know that?
Alien: We are linked to each other.

Question: Linked? How?
With what?
What kind of link?
Alien: Our Cellular Motor.

Question: Here we go again with this crap of.... (Lines erased, unreadable.)
Note: Second line was smeared.
Question: Can you forget for a second about your Cellular Motor, and explain how the link is established between you and your people? It is by telepathy?

89

Alien: Not always.
You need telepathy only when others don't receive your direct message, or understand your thoughts' projection.

Question: Are you willing to teach us your language?
Alien: It is worthless on Earth.

Question: Why?
Alien: It does not correspond to anything you have on Earth.

Question: What would happen if one of us lands on your planet?
Alien: He will die.

Question: Why?
Alien: The atmosphere.

Question: Please explain.
Alien: Humans can't survive on our planet.
Before they arrive to our planet, they will be crashed, they will melt, they will be vaporized.

Question: By what?
Who will melt them?
Alien: Cosmic radiations.

Question: If we manage to escape radiations or wear protective suits, and land on your planet, what would happen to us?
More bad surprises...
Alien: You will suffocate.

Question: Why?
Alien: No oxygen.
No atmosphere. And you will loose all your senses.

Question: We will carry oxygen tanks and special equipments.
Alien: They will stop to function. You and your equipments will float like feathers. You will not be able to land.

Question: If I remember you told us that part of your planet has an atmosphere, so we will land there.
Alien: First, you have to penetrate the non-atmosphere zone.
Second, you must survive the non-atmosphere zone, which you can't...It would take you millions of years. And if you succeed to do so, you will have no more muscles left; no more bones, no more blood, and no more tissues.

Question: Do you have a chronology of Earth?
Alien: It is recorded.

Question: Where?
Alien: in the Miraya.

Question: What is that?
Alien: A cosmic monitor. A cosmic depository.

Question: Where do we find this depository?
Alien: You can't. It is beyond your reach.

Question: Who recorded Earth's chronology?
Alien: You did. Everuting you did; your noise, your broadcast, your wars, your savagery, your weapons, your violence.

Question: We did?
How could we, if the depository you talked about is beyond our reach?
Alien: You could still look at some far distant objects or at a particular destination and you would not be able to reach any of these objects and the far away destination you are looking at, because of the enormous distances that separate them from you, but they will always be there, whether you reach them or not.
You do not need to reach a destination or touch an object to make it exist. Look at your moon. Did you reach it?
No. But it is there. Same thing for the depository.
It is there like the Moon which you can't reach, maybe in the future, you will land on the surface of the Moon, and you will begin to understand.

Question: Would you feel my hand if I touch you?
Alien: It will register.

Question: Meaning what?
Alien: My Cellular Motor will first sense what you feel when you touch me.

Question: Please explain.
Alien: As soon as you touch my "Frame", my Cellular Motor registers everything about your hand.
It will read your health condition, your intentions, your emotions, your strength, your weaknesses; anything and everything your hand can release. This is what our Essence will sense and feel.

Question: You mean you would feel what I would normally feel if I touch you? My own feelings?
Physical feelings?
Alien: Yes.

Question: If so, then you do not have personal feelings?
Alien: Our Essence has more feelings than you can imagine.
We understand physical feelings.
We are not affected by physical feelings because we are NOT biological. Our Frame receives and our Cellular Motor reads and analyses instantly.

Question: Do you sense danger?
Do you feel pain?
Do you feel heat and cold?
Alien: We do. We also feel what is not physical.
This is more important.
You do not have enough energy to leave a lasting impression.
Do not confuse energy with physical strength or a violent act.
Physical strength does not affect us.
And a violent act is instantly neutralized by our Essence.

Question: What kind of memory do you have?
Alien: Non-sensorial memory.

Question: Please explain.
Alien: Cellular memory.

Question: What is a Cellular Memory?
Alien: It is everything.
It is an essential and original part of the basic mechanism of our Cellular Motor. It contains and constantly updates our depot of knowledge, our learning, and analyzes what to anticipate.

Question: Where is located your memory?
Alien: It is collective.
It is shared.
It is transmitted.
It has no determined location.
But it is animated by a center in our Cellular Motor.

Question: Is your Cellular Motor an engine?
A motor in the real sense?
Alien: To a certain degree. But it is Not organic.
It is not biological.
It is not physical.

Question: Do you have a written language?
Alien: Yes, affirmative.
Question: Is it the same for all the people who live up there?

Alien: Up there?
Note: The linguist used the words "People", and "Up there".

Question: And everybody understands your language?
Alien: Yes, affirmative.
(Note: On the screen of the speaking device, this answer changed color to deep pink, instantly. I don't know the meaning of this sudden change in color from black to pink.)

Question: Do you use a well-defined alphabet?
Alien: We have created what you call "Alphabet".

Question: What do you mean?
Please explain in terms and words we can understand.
Alien: Our written alphabet is not very different from the early alphabet of the Phoenicians. But it is richer scientifically.

Question: Please explain this.
Alien: Our alphabet is scientifically created to correspond to all aspects and forms of science and our knowledge of the universe.

Question: What do you mean?
Alien: The truth in the universe should be expressed through one universal language that could be easily and rapidly understood by other civilizations, from the past, the present and the future, even though, the three are one.

Question: Again, please explain what do you mean?
Alien: You will not understand now. None of you will.

Question: Is your alphabet used in math, chemistry and physics?
Alien: It is one unified language for all our knowledge, including science and other forms of learning.

Question: Why didn't you learn English?
Alien: It is insignificant. It is limited. It is too little.

Question: Do you know, speak or understand any other Earth's language (s)?
Alien: It is insignificant. It is limited. It is too little.

Question: Do you understand anything...about....
Note: Few lines and dots could not be read.
our language, vocabulary, phrases, or writings....?
Note: The question did not end here; the last two lines could not be read, because of missing ink.
Alien: Yes.

Question: Is your alphabet or language purely scientific?
Alien: Yes.

Question: Do you express emotions in your language?
Aliens: Emotions is not the right word. Instead we use the word "Intelligence".

Question: What intelligence has to do with emotions when we are talking about language compositions and vocabulary?
Alien: Emotions are humans' natural responses and reactions to many things.
We do not react, we act.
We do not respond, we continue the process.

Question: What do you mean? Please explain.
Alien: You will not understand.
Note: The general stepped in.

The general's question: Is there some sort of a secret language or a code you use when you communicate with other groups?
By the way how do you communicate with others?
Alien: No code. No secrets.
No hidden language in any of our communications.
Knowledge is universally shared.

General's question: Do you talk to each other?
What language do you use?
Can we learn your language?
Alien: Yes affirmative.
We use a cosmic scientific knowledge understood by all recipients.
Yes you can learn our language. It is simple. It is complete.
It is truthful. It is infinite.

General's question: Who are those recipients?
Alien: The Essences.

General's question: The Essences? Meaning what?
Who? Who are these essences?
Alien: Everything and anything that has intelligence.
Note: I am absolutely sure that the General did not understand what the alien meant.

This lack or inability of understanding the alien became apparent in additional questions the General asked much later, and which I can't print in this book, because they relate to military secrets and national security.

General's question: Are the signs, the symbols and geometric shapes and drawings on your craft from your language?
Alien: Yes. Affirmative.

General's question: What do they mean?
Alien: You have the same thing on your flying machines.

General's question: What same thing? What? What?
What are you talking about?
Alien: Look at the screen.
(Note: The alien meant the speaking device.)

General's question: How can we learn your language?
Do you have manuals? Books?
Alien: No books.

General's question: So how can we learn it then?
Alien: You will, when we feel you are ready and worthy.
Note: This was not the end of the meeting.
Additional subjects pertaining to weapons, military strategies, and national security were discussed.

*** *** ***

Aliens', summary of findings from and about:
What we do know from aliens.
What we do know about aliens.
Facts:
Summary of findings
References/Sources:
AT: Aliens' Transcripts
OR: Official reports

1. Our government met with three different non-human species with an exceptional intelligence, and highly advanced technology and science.
According to official documents, reports and meetings with aliens' transcripts, these three species are:
a-An intraterrestrial non-human race that lived on Earth for millions of years. Originally from Zeta Reticuli, this race is known to the general public as the Greys or the Grays; a reference or possibly a descriptive definition given by people who claimed that they have been abducted by the Grays, and/or have encountered them.
Official records/reports refer to them as Biological Entities, Space Monkeys, Shorty Aliens, EBE, Aliens. They are also known as intra-terrestrials because they have their habitats "inside Earth", underwater, as well as on remote areas inaccessible to us. This race was mentioned numerous times in the Aliens Transcripts
b-Anunnaki; wrongly defined as those who came to Earth from above. They are of an extra-terrestrial origin, but did not come from Nibiru, which is an Akkadian and a Chaldean name for Jupiter. Their constellation is called Ashta.Ri. Our governments met only twice with the Anunnaki who interestingly enough, were represented by two females. This race was mentioned 14 times in the Aliens Transcripts. AT; OR
c-Naftarian race, because allegedly they came from the Star System called Naftari, yet to be discovered and acknowledged by mainstream science. Official records show that our governments did meet with the Naftarians on many occasions for a very long time. And the first meeting occurred in 1947. This race was mentioned numerous times in the Aliens Transcripts, because of the vital scientific information and instructions we received from the Naftarians. Some were extremely useful when their principles were tested and applied by military scientists. On this, my lips are sealed. AT; OR
2. Some governments have an illustrated catalogue of various and numerous non-human and extraterrestrial races scattered in the immensity of the Cosmos.

The drawings and illustrations of their anatomy, physiology and physiognomy were based upon information given to us by the Grays.

Our knowledge of outer-of-space entities comes directly from the Grays and a lengthy report by an Anunnaki. So far, none of these extraterrestrial entities contacted us. We do not have sufficient or meaningful information and scientific data about any of them. Some, for reasons we don't know or we don't understand, have visited planet Earth, thousands of years ago, and never returned.

According to the aliens we met with and previously mentioned here, and in the Aliens' Transcripts, galactic civilizations are not interested in us, as simple as that. OR

Why? Because some are millions and others billions of years ahead of us.

3. The alien who survived the UFO crash near Roswell was a female. She was detained by the authorities for a few months, and later on died in custody. She was not a "Gray", but a hybrid.

She was able to communicate with us in English. And she had a "functional mouth" and human characteristics and features, such as senses, reactions, and emotional behavior. She did not look at all like the other Grays-Aliens who died in the crash. OR

4. The Grays-Aliens who died in the UFO crash near Roswell did not have internal organs similar to ours; they had no heart, no blood circulatory system, no mouth, no ears, etc. And we found out from autopsy of their dead bodies that they had a bizarre green liquid inside their bodies.

Some experts in the field claimed that the green fluid substituted for blood, but such claim was never confirmed by mainstream science and medical sciences. OR

5. Contrary to a general belief, the Grays-Aliens do not always communicate with us, and especially with abductees and/or contactees, telepathically. Many of them are capable of speaking in English. This was confirmed by official reports. AT; OR

6. Two very influential American Catholic Archbishops were instrumental in shaping non-disclosure policies about the UFOs crash near Roswell and dissemination of information about the existence of extraterrestrials.

Both were Archbishops of New York.

1-Francis Joseph Cardinal Spellman
2-Terence James Cardinal Cooke. OR

Cardinal Spellman

Cardinal Cooke

Reverend Billy Graham

7. Reverend Billy Graham was officially consulted by two American Presidents on extraterrestrials' affairs, nature, and encounters. He shared the opinions of the Catholic prelates and recommended that the aliens' question should not be discussed publicly, and any pertinent information should be handled in utmost secrecy, fearing public's mass hysteria. OR

8. An unauthorized copy of the Aliens Transcripts was sent to Pope Pius XII, Abba Eban (Member of the American Academy of Sciences. Israel's Deputy Prime Minister, Minister of Education and Culture, Minister of Foreign Affairs) and David Ben Gurion (First Prime Minister of Israel).

Dag Hammarskjöld, (UN Secretary-General 1953-61) request for a copy of the AT was turned down by the military. OR

Pope Pius XII

Abba Eban.

David Ben Gurion. First President of the State of Israel.

Dag Hammarskjöld, UN Secretary-General 1953-61.

9.None of the aliens (Grays) who met with our governments had reproductive organs, a human respiratory system, and a digestive system.
All of them told us that they do not consume food, and do not have waste inside their bodies, except an Anunnaki who said that her race consume human and non-human food, but they dispose of the waste through an internal gland capable of eliminating any absorbed substance, solid or liquid. OR; AT

10.The internal structure of the aliens' bodies is animated by a cellular motor located in the brain, called Cellular Motor. And the brain is not biological or organic.
It is purely cellular consisting of intricate cells channels and mental-electrical frequencies circuit. The aliens' brain does not produce emotions, but it recognizes them as mental images. OR; AT

11.The aliens do not have a nervous system. Thus, they do not physically feel pain, stress, anxiety, fatigue, hunger, heat, cold, and similar reactions/sensations/feelings/symptoms. OR; AT

12.The intraterrestrials have three long and skinny fingers on each hand. The non-human races from Ashtari and Naftari have five fingers on each hand, just like us. OR; AT

13.None of the aliens we have met hasd a retina. OR; AT

14.Aliens from highly advanced civilizations have multiple copies of their "Essences" (Body frame, being, mental-physical structure, etc.)
In other words, authentic copies of their bodies with astonishing space-time memory capabilities. OR; AT

15.The salty waters of our seas and oceans are frequently used by the intraterrestrials as fuel for their crafts. OR; AT

16.Aliens' spacecrafts don't need maintenance and repair.
They are "re-serviced", and kept in an excellent condition by scanning machines that recharge their propulsion system, balance their anti-gravity/zooming in-zooming out system, and eliminates metal-fatigue. OR; AT

17.Almost all aliens' spacecrafts are directly linked to the mind (Brain/Cellular Motor) of the alien pilots.

They do not have dashboards, gears, navigation system, or any of the landing and take-off tools we find on our crafts. The alien pilot becomes one of the craft he/she/it piloting, and vice versa.

In some instances and conditions, the aliens' spacecraft flight (More precisely Jump, zooming in, and zooming out, and penetrating time-space pockets) receives commands from a head-band tied around the alien pilot's skull, or worn around the forehead. OR; AT

18.Aliens and intraterrestrials do not give individuals, so-called contactees and abductees, personal messages to be delivered to humanity.

Aliens and intraterrestrials rarely talk to abductees, almost never; no reason to. In some rare instances, they express "something" by slowly and gradually raising their hands or directly staring at individuals, who are usually in a state of shock, fear, confusion, and paralysis. OR

19.The so-called telepathic communication between an alien, an intraterrestrial and so-called contactees and abductees is a very rare phenomenon.

It only occurs when the individual is an exceptionally alert person, who remains coherent, and does not succumb to panic and emotional disturbances, and does not fall into a state of paralysis. OR

20.The words "sex", and "intercourse" do not exist in the aliens' vocabulary. Not even once, any of these two words were ever used by an alien during any meeting.

Although, they are very familiar with how we reproduce and how human sexual behavior conditions and influences our lifestyle and habits. OR

21.Not all aliens have the same vocabulary. There are millions of galactic languages and dialects.

However, there is a universal/cosmic protocol language used and understood by millions of galactic civilizations. OR; AT

22. Aliens' bodies do not have body odors. Only, when the body of an intraterrestrial or a hybrid has been autopsied, a very strong and suffocating smell comes out from inside the body.

Usually, it comes out, when a green fluid suddenly emerges from the internal organs which are extremely different from ours.

During an "aliens' autopsy", none of the operating surgeons and nurses inside the autopsy room could stand the smell. They ran away "like a mad dog" said one of the military nurses.
In fact, the odor was so strong, it invaded the whole compound. They had to seal the room for 24 hours. Physicians at Walter Reed Army Medical Center, became very concerned and alarmed, for they sought that the smell could be very toxic. OR

Note: Worth mentioning here that no autopsy report from Walter Reed was ever issued by a physician (Pathologist) who conducted any kind of autopsy on dead aliens.
Instead, scattered and reconstructed medical notes (Unsigned) were sent to the Pentagon two days later.
This is not a normal military or medical procedure as any one might guess. But it did happen intentionally, and I am unable to elaborate further on this situation.

The names of the pathologists and assisting nurses were never revealed to "outsider-civilians".
And the preliminary notes vanished from the face of the earth. Thus, there is no way to honestly and accurately document the autopsy. And most certainly, the autopsy was not filmed.
I am absolutely certain that no civilian or any officer below the rank of Colonel had access to any autopsy report. Even at the Pentagon, only two generals and one military surgeon had access to a medical report describing in details the anatomy and physiology of the aliens. Said report was then submitted to The White House.
To the best of my knowledge, there is only one original report which remained hidden somewhere in a secret military dossier at The Pentagon, and one copy of the report which was read by the President and YES disposed of. Grosso modo, and quite honestly, we don't know a thing about the aliens' autopsy. Yes, it did happen, but there are no records to substantiate the fact that it did happen.

23.The dead bodies of the aliens recovered from the UFO crash near Roswell were not shipped to Washington in wooden boxes filled with dry-ice, but in heavy and tick glass container filled with chemicals and containing a blue liquid. The glass container was placed inside a large wooden box.

It went directly to Walter Reed, and not to a military base in Roswell or anywhere else, and for sure, the box containing the bodies of dead aliens was not stored in a military hangar in Roswell or at any other military base/facility.

Clear and firm orders came from Washington to ship the "Container" right away to Walter Reed. OR

24.The aliens we met could not walk straight and in a balanced manner, because they did not have muscles to support their weight, even though, they were very miniscule and frail.

Nevertheless their hands were very flexible and agile. Only two species could walk gracefully; the Anunnaki and the Naftarians. The hybrids walked just like us.

And some were tall by aliens' standards. However, they could not move their head right and left without twisting their body. It appeared to us as if their neck was barely attached to their head.

This is one of the easily recognized features/characteristics of the Grays-Hybrids.

25.In addition to the brass, psychiatrists, neurologists and teams of scientists who questioned the aliens, few anthropologists and historians were allowed to attend some meetings and ask the aliens questions pertaining to the history of human civilization, and various early humans settlements in different parts of the world.

I found their interest in these subjects very refreshing, since they explore the very core and very foundation of our history's birth and development.

A professor from Harvard asked the aliens about the first human settlement on Earth, and our ancestors' use of early tools.

Another professor from Yale asked about the early form of human communities in Africa and the Middle East.

A third from Princeton asked about the veracity of historical texts carved on clay tablets and slabs.

And another university professor from Pennsylvania asked about the first established (systematic/organized) human community in Mesopotamia.

The aliens told us a lot about our origin, the customs, habits and way of life of the earliest organized human communities.

For instance, the aliens told us that our history did not start in Mesopotamia but in Turkey.

The aliens meant by that, a well-civilized human community, but they made it clear to us that the first human settlement that can be described as a "a human cell or community" started some 120,000 years ago, in pre-history, during the Middle Palaeolithic Period in Barda Balka and Hazar Merd in ancient Iraq.

A regional flood in the Middle East wiped them out and decimated their habitats. Then the alien continued to tell us that during the Upper Palaeolithic Period, some 35,000 ago, another human civilization came to life in Zarzi, Palegawra and other regions of Northern Iraq, particularly in the upper region of Kurdistan Zagros Mountains.

Concurrently, very advanced human communities flourished in Phoenicia and Northern part of Anatolia.

Asking the aliens whether extraterrestrials had any influence in speeding up the process of human evolution, languages and intelligence, and understanding of nature, and the aliens said, yes, but only in some parts of Earth.

The aliens told us for instance that the early humans did not look human at all. Some walked on three legs, others on four legs like animals; they could not talk, they could not reason, and they could not understand their environment, but had an enormous physical strength, endurance, and could see things very far away, and hear better than many of the animals of their time. Their eyes were their primordial and principle tool of communication with each others, animals and nature. A highly advanced galactic race from Ashta.Ri Constellation System came to Earth and upgraded existing human-animal species they captured in Central Africa and the Amazon area in Brazil.

Early humans or pre-historic humans-animals species were not aware that other species like them lived in different part of Earth.

108

Approximately 110,000 year old Palaeolithic stone used as an axe.

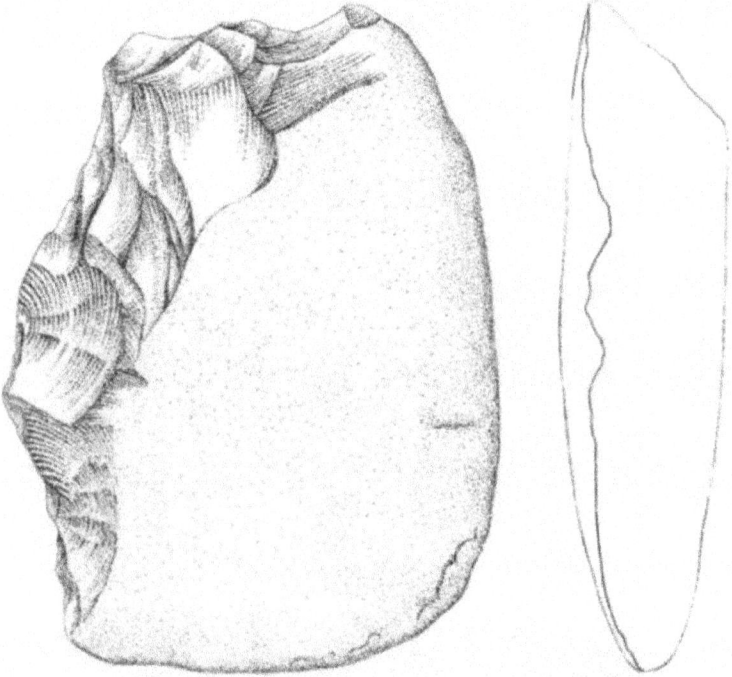

A Lower Paleolithic Period stone-chopper found in
Anatolia/Turkey.

Shanidar Cave area in Iraq, where our earliest ancestors lived, and Neanderthal remains were discovered.

And contrary to our general belief they did not migrate from one continent to another, told us the aliens. Some of the early human species were not very much different from the Modern Man, only those who lived in Central Africa, Brazil, South-East Asia were very different from other quasi-human species because they were not totally humans.

Our early (Earliest is more accurate) ancestors who lived in Mesopotamia during the Pre-Historic Palaeolithic Period looked very different from those who lived in Africa and Brazil and surrounding areas.

Numerous human and quasi-human forms, species and life-forms existed and co-exited on Earth. Only those who were genetically upgraded or "modified" by extraterrestrials survived, developed and influenced the course of history and human civilizations. The aliens referred to the early inhabitants of Turkey-Anatolia, Phoenicia, and Mesopotamia, modern day Iraq. They did not even mention the early Egyptians.

Thus, the Theory "Out-of-Africa" is wrong! AT

26. A huge flood did occur in antiquity (Pre-Biblical time), but it was not global and did not cover the entire Earth. It was regional and it did decimate habitats, villages and settlements, only in the Middle East. The Biblical story of the Deluge is not correct. And there is no such thing as Noah Arch, as written in the Bible. AT
Note: This part of the aliens' revelations was never mentioned in any official report for obvious reasons.
27.Not all aliens are short with three fingers on each hand.
On some planets, galactic beings do not have fingers at all, not even hands. Many of our human body features and organs are useless on other planets. Eyes, hands, fingers and our five senses are not needed. AT
28.Contrary to a common and popular belief in ufology's circles and New Age thoughts/Schools milieus, aliens do not talk about spirituality, the Saints, God, Jesus and other prophets.
But it did happen a few times, when some abductees asked the aliens about God, heaven, hell, the final judgment, reincarnation, and the return of Jesus Christ.
Aliens are not concerned with religious spirituality, for they do not have a religion.
An alien told us that the idea of God was created when the first quasi-intelligent being discovered fire; the early humans called fire "God".
Fire was the first god or supernatural power they worshipped, followed by the stars. AT
Note: This part of the aliens' revelations was never mentioned in any official report.

29.In virtue of some passages taken from official reports but never mentioned in the AT (Aliens' Transcripts), one of the most knowledgeable persons on the subjects of extraterrestrials, alien abduction, and their spacecrafts is President George Bush Sr.; he had a direct access to the Aliens Transcripts, Top Secret and Above Top Secret reports, studies and testimonies from civilians and the military (army senior officers, air force commanders and pilots), and other semi-official and governmental agencies.

While serving as Director of the Central Intelligence Agency (CIA), President Bush gathered and reviewed the world most detailed and documented reports and findings on aliens' spacecrafts, their technology, and extraterrestrials, including their interactions with a few human beings.

Former President George Bush Sr. was and still is one of the world's most knowledgeable persons on the subjects of extraterrestrials. President Bush was the Director of Central Intelligence and head of the Central Intelligence Agency from 30 January 1976 to 20 January 1977.

While serving as Director of the Central Intelligence Agency (CIA), President Bush gathered and reviewed the world most detailed and documented reports and findings on aliens' spacecrafts, their technology, and extraterrestrials, including their interactions with a few human beings.

113

President George Bush's files on UFOs and extraterrestrials are nowhere to be found. But they DID exist!

It was never the intention of the CIA to mislead the general public on matters and issues related to alien technology, the UFO phenomena, and other pertinent subjects. Misleading was NOT the CIA objective.

The CIA quite rightfully and legally withheld delicate information on these subjects because revealing such information and declassifying files will absolutely jeopardize national security, the safety, and sanity of the American people, as well as many people around the globe.

It was not the CIA which decided to keep the UFO question an Above Top Secret matter, but two powerful (Former) Presidents, and an extremely influential committee/panel consisting of Archbishops, the nations' leading scientists, and commanding generals from the army and the air force.

30.According to one alien, the first four human civilizations on Earth with social structure on many levels were:

1-Those who lived during the Ubaid Period. And this can be easily documented by archeological excavations, artifacts and historical findings.

Those people had nothing to do with extraterrestrials.

Many authors attempted to link them to extraterrestrials and particularly to the Anunnaki, Igigi and Lemurians. Such attempts are colorful but were never based upon scientific, historical and archeological facts. And those who did so were not familiar with Old Babylonian, Akkadian and Sumero-Assyrian languages.

2-Those who lived in ancient Turkey/Anatolia, more precisely in Cappadocia. The extraterrestrials influenced their way of life, beliefs, and especially their architecture. Unfortunately and regrettably, our knowledge of their civilization and communities is very limited.

3-Those who lived near Lake Van and on the high plateau of pre-historic Armenia.

4-The very early inhabitants of the lands, islands and shores of Phoenicia, at the time these lands had no name.

Ubaid figurine (5,000-5,600 B.C., Mesopotamia.)
Unfortunately, many misinformed authors in the West claimed
that this figurine depicts an extraterrestrial reptilian race.
Rubbish!

Ubaid orpoles.

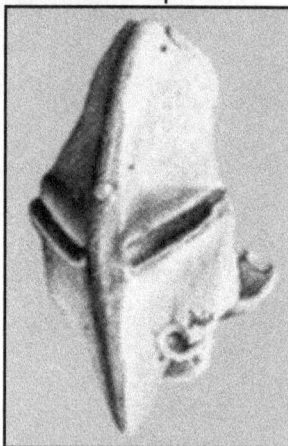
Ubaid artifact.

Again, and regrettably, some very popular authors and ufology's enthusiasts in the West have claimed that the Ubaid artifact depicts the face or an extraterrestrial race, referred to as reptilians, Anunnaki and even the Grays, and aliens from Zeta Reticuli. This is not the case at all.

Even though the face features, and particularly the shape of the eyes are odd by humans standards. Even an amateur archeologist will mock such ridiculous claims.

116

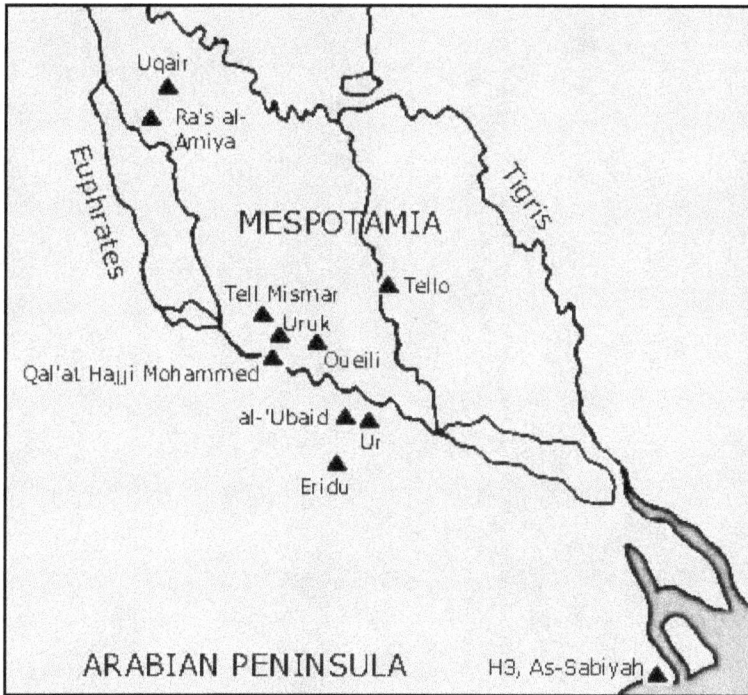

Map of the location of Al Ubaid and ancient Mesopotamian cities.
Sumerian scribes claimed that Eridu (Their own city) is the oldest city on Earth. The truth is this: The Al-Ubaid region is the oldest city-settlement-habitat-community in Mesopotamia.

Cappadocia: The Fairy Chimeys.

This area was called Mt. Argeus and nicknamed the Abode of the Gods. According to the aliens, this region witnessed the daw of human civilization on Earth. So, our history books are wrong.

Cappadocia today.
Elaborate underground tunnels are still accessible to us.

Map of ancient Anatolia.

Pre-historic Armenian Obelisks.

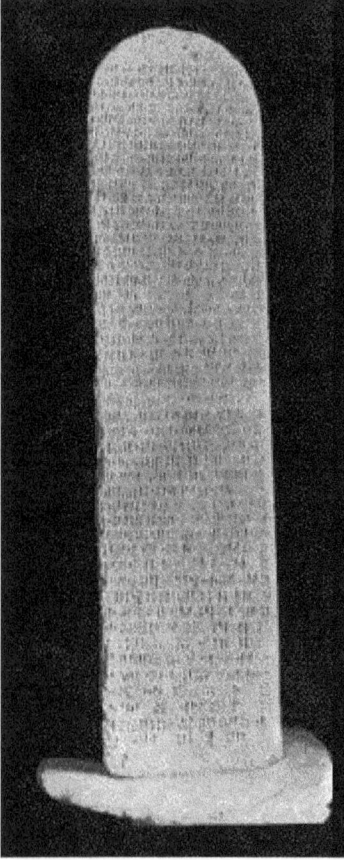

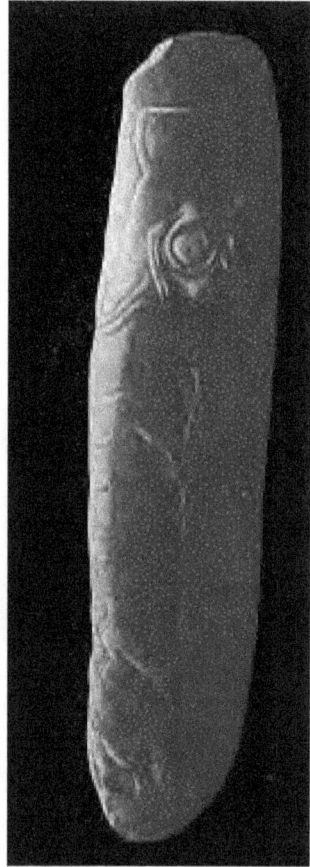

Armenian Vishapakar, "Dragon Stone" with characters belonging
to an unknown language, and which resembles some of the
letters of the Ana'kh (Anunnaki language) ca. 1200 B.C.

Lake Van area; a primordial part of the cradle of human civilization on Earth.

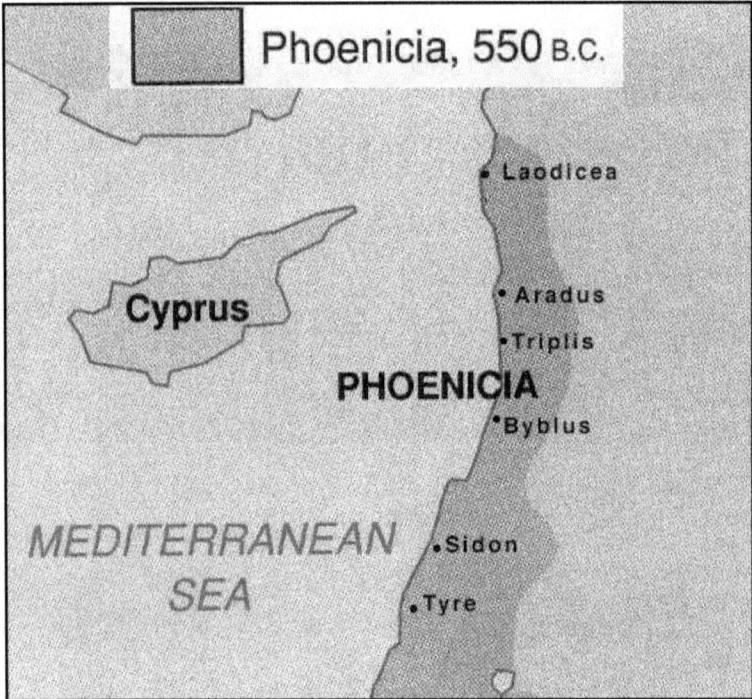

Map of Phoenicia, 550 B.C.
Tyre, Sidon, Byblus and Aradus were Anunnaki colonies on Earth.

Map showing the locations and borders of Phoenicia, Anatolia, Mesopotamia, Ancient Turkey, and the high plateau of Ancient Armenia; all these regions were visited by the Anunnaki. (Extraterrestrials or mythical Mesopotamian deities... it does not make any difference!)

Ancient cities that were referred to as the cradle of civilization, and part of the kingdom of the Anunnaki on Earth were (As shown on this map);

Palmyra

Arados

Ugarit

Tyre

Sidon

Cyprus,

Babylon (Mesopotamia)

Anatolia

Lycia

Cilicia

Urartu

Rhode

Karatepe

Dr. von Braun (in the center) talking with T. Keith Glennan, second from right, the first Administrator of NASA.
From L to R: Delmar Morris, Deputy Director Administration for the Marshall Center, Dr. Eberhard Rees, Deputy Director for Research and Development for the Marshall Center, Dr. Von Braun, T. Keith Glennan, Don Ostrander, NASA launch vehicle chief.
They knew a lot about extraterrestrials' spacecrafts and aliens. They were among the first administrators to review the Aliens'Transcripts.

Dr. Von Braun with members of his management team, 1960.

From L to R: Werner Kuers, Director of the Manufacturing Engineering Division, Dr. Walter Haeussermann, Director of the Astrionics Division, Dr. William Mrazek, Propulsion and Vehicle Engineering Division, Dr. Von Braun, Dieter Grau, Director of the Quality Assurance Division, Dr. Oswald Lange, Director of the Saturn Systems Office, and Erich Neubert, Associate Deputy Director for Research and Development.
All worked on aliens' reverse engineering, except Dieter Grau.

———————————————

Dr. Robert Seamans, Associate NASA Administrator with
Dr. Von Braun testifying before space-related congressional
committees in 1961.
Dr. Seamans is very familiar with the Aliens Transcripts.

**Excerpts from other meetings with aliens which
occurred years later.**

Habitable planet or an Earth-like planet:
The alien said that "Jamara" is the name of one of three stars from
Barach-shimsu system (We call it Alpha Centauri system) which
sustains life as we know it.
It is 4.37 light years away from Earth. It is like your planet. It has
atmosphere, water, forest, rivers, mountains, volcanos. It has
sweet and salty liquid water on and under the surface. You can't
reach it." AT.

Note: The word "Jamara" was later shortened by the military to
"Jam 1." Very appropriate!!!
6 months after NASA was established (1960), a mini-copy (Sent
as a report) of this particular transcript was sent to:
a-T. Keith Glennan, NASA first administrator, and Dr. Robert
Seamans, Associate NASA Administrator.
b-Wilbur Brucker, then United States Army Secretary.
Dr. von Braun, Dr. Oswald Lange, Major General John Barclay,
and Dr. William Mrazek, Propulsion and Vehicle Engineering
Division (Dr. von Braun's scientific team) read the transcript
before it was sent to Mr. Glennan.

Earth is the universe's dumpster:
Asking an alien (For the third time between 1947 and 1951) about
what do exraterrestrial civilizations think of the people of Earth,
and the alien replied: "Your planet is the dumpster of the universe
(Referring to one universe, not multiple universes, or other
universes, or the whole universe). Undesirable life-forms (Like
beings and similar entities) on several planets, when punished, are
sent to Earth. Some look like you. Some don't."
Then we asked the alien, "You mean a non-human race from
outer-space actually lives here on Earth?"
The alien replied: "Yes".
A third question followed, "Where did they come from and where
do they live now on Earth?"

129

The alien replied: "They were expelled from Planet "Saphribeh", and they live on your planet, underwater, inside Earth and on remtre areas you have not reached yet."

Question: What is Saphribeh and where it is located?

Answer of the alien: "Name of their place (A binary star system we call Zeta Reticuli) which is 39 light-years away from your planet. You can't reach it." AT.

Note: The word "Saphribeh" was later shortened by the military to "Saf." Very appropriate!!!

"How long it took them (The expelled aliens) to get here?" we asked. And the alien replied: "A few hours."

Note: Nobody in the room believed the alien except one already famous science-fiction writer.

6 months after NASA was established (1960), a mini-copy (Sent as a report) of this particular transcript was sent to T. Keith Glennan, NASA first administrator. Dr. von Braun read the transcript before it was sent to Mr. Glennan

Aliens' reproduction and the "Productive Essence":
The female alien interrogated by Americans, had feminine features, but did not look like a female. In two paragraphs from the Aliens Transcripts, it was noted that the word "Female" was incorrectly used by one interpreter.

When the alien referred to herself as a female, linguistically and anatomically she meant "A productive Essence". In the aliens' world, it is her "type" which created life, produced and reproduced life-forms without the help (Sexually) of an alien mate.

Riyah, the female alien told us that the aliens produce, reproduce and give birth to life-forms (aka Essence, Being, Creature) through a scientific process incomprehensible to us.

Manufactured aliens: The aliens' essences (creatures) are given life instantly and they are complete when they are born (Produced). In other words, they do not need years upon years to become adult and mature. They are born adult with all the knowledge, wisdom and information they need to function as a complete, fully grown, fully developed, fully intelligent creatures.

Aliens' Transcripts (AT):

I.Definition:
The Aliens' Transcripts (AT) are a collection, a record, a detailed account, a huge dossier on all the meetings with non-human entities that occurred from 1947 to the present.

The Aliens' Transcripts have a paramount military significance and an enormous national security importance.

The Aliens' Transcripts (AT) contain thousands upon thousands of pages, sketches, illustrations, charts, graphs, communiqués, notes, statistics, secret Presidential orders, addenda, revised, and re-revised and updated addenda on everything pertaining to encounters and meetings with aliens.

However, the AT do not include civilians' encounters with aliens, abductions or UFOs' sightings.

AT are strictly and exclusively transcripts of meetings with aliens, extraterrestrials, and intraterrestrials.

From mid to the end of 1947, the Aliens Transcripts were a straight documentation and minutes of meetings with aliens in general; extraterrestrials, and intraterrestrials (The Grays).

In 1948, the Air Force and the Pentagon jointly decided to divide the Transcripts into three categories or parts, and as follows:

Category one/Part One: The meetings. This category recorded all questions and answers, and what it was decided upon to do or to continue to do during the meetings.

The minutes contained all the topics and subjects discussed, the material studied, and especially those of a military and scientific nature, names, ranks and titles of people (military and civilians) who were present, followed by recommendations and brief reports from scientists.

Issues, discussions and subjects on religion, ethics, Earth history, and anthropology were later incorporated in category three/part three. This decision was made by a two stars general following studies and reports submitted to his office by a committee of physicians, psychiatrists, and experts in behavioral sciences, who at the time, were working on esoteric, mind control, and psychosomatic projects and research.

131

Category two/Part Two: The projects:
This category refers to research programs, projects, and training sessions administered by two offices especially created by the military and The White House. In this category, detailed reports on "Progress" were submitted by trusted military contractors, and added to the Transcripts. On this, my lips are sealed.

Category three/Part Three: Addenda and reports. This category gathered and catalogued all sorts of information on aliens':
1-Nature.
2-Races.
3-Species.
4-Origin.
5-Habitat.
6-Technology.
7-Future operations.
8-Reports from military personnel at all levels on their personal rapports with aliens who worked with them in military bases.
9-Study and analysis of the behavior of the aliens.
10-Habits.
11-Strengths and weaknesses.
12-Nutrition.
13-Reactions in confined places.
14-Reactions/attitudes under severe weather conditions (Cold and heat).
15-Confrontations and debates with scientists, the military, and military guards.
16-Flights' tests.
17-Reverse engineering, so on.

Who had or has access to these transcripts?
Even 4 star generals could not access these transcripts. President ...tried and failed. Senator...did everything he could to have a glance at AT and he was "sent away". Vice President...inquired about AT, and he was told, there is no such thing as Aliens' Transcripts. A congressional hearing was scheduled to inquire about AT and conduct some sort of questioning, deposition and investigation, but 2 two days later, it was cancelled.

Rudolf Schriever

In 1950, Rudolf Schriever, a highly respected German engineer told *Der Spiegel* magazine that, he had designed a 49 feet in diameter circular flying aircraft. Schriever also claimed that a BMW's engineering team designed and manufactured one of the first Nazi UFO prototypes.

In 1945, he was in charge of the UFOs' production, and in April of the same year, he fled to Czechoslovakia. In the fifties, he joined the German-American scientists' team working in the United States.

At one time, Dr. Hynek tried to have access to the Transcripts and the Pentagon said: NO!
But Dr. Werhner von Braun, Dr. Edward Teller, Dr. Oberth, Albert Einstein, two young German scientists who are still around (They worked with Viktor Schauberger), and a young and brilliant scientist (Still alive) who worked with the late Karl Schapeller, had plenty of time and opportunities to go through the files of the Transcripts.
In 1948, we heard that Rudolph Schriever joined the scientists' team, although some colleagues have claimed that Schriever never participated in any project, simply because he died that year in Czechoslovakia. In 1951, Alberto Fenoglio, joined the team.
Twenty years later, Dr. Carl Sagan, and a very famous scientist (Still alive) known for his mind-bending theory on galactic civilizations were added to the roster.

*** *** ***

A file from the Aliens' Transcripts which was shared with NASA, USAF, The White House, and NSA:
Note: This file contains information and summary of findings already mentioned in previous sections of the book. However, it includes new items which were not revealed or itemized in other reports and transcripts I included in this work.

According to notes in the transcripts, Section 9: Addendum 12-Briefing 341-E1, 1947, this first encounter/meeting was arranged by an alien who was in the custody of the Air Force.
At the bottom of the page, there is an arrow and a reference made to a certain "Lt. Colonel S..." On the next page, top left, the words or phrase "No outfits" was mentioned.
The alien stayed at a military base for approximately 3 months and 4 days, and later died. Her body was sent to a military hospital. The alien was captured after her spacecraft crashed, for missing to "jump" into the time-space pocket, needed to enter and exit a physical dimension. The three other aliens died on impact. The one who survived was a female alien-hybrid, although no genital organs were visible (I will talk about this, later on.)

So, apparently, the aliens did something to their spacecraft, so radiations emitted by their ships would not affect us, or perhaps, they totally eliminated any radioactive emission.

The aliens told us to warn our people not to come close to any of their spacecrafts when they land unannounced (In all cases and other circumstances), because their spacecrafts' radiations cause temporary loss of memory, nausea, vomiting, severe headaches, temporary paralysis, temporary loss of sight, and severe skin burns.

By the way, they call their spacecrafts "Time-Space machines", because they don't fly, but jump from one time-space pocket to another. Worth mentioning here, that the Russians upon meeting the aliens for the first time, did wear special suits, for protection measures. The suits were manufactured in Tbilisi, Georgia, former state of the Soviet Union, and the suits were stored at Kapustin Yar.

The transcripts revealed in no particular order:

1. Aliens cannot constantly breathe oxygen; they will suffocate and die.

2. Almost all aliens are claustrophobic. They will be disoriented if they are confined in a small area for a certain period of time in the same place.

3. There are 224 planets that sustain life as we know it.

4. Four other galactic species including the Anunnaki and Igigi resemble humans to a certain degree.

5. Two governments have a huge dossier cataloguing alien species by category, type, class, faculty, intelligence, science, technology, physiognomy, nature, and location of their habitat.

6. Aliens don't have genitals; they don't reproduce sexually.

7. Aliens don't have a digestive system.

8. Aliens don't have a retina.

9. Aliens don't have a centralized nervous system.

10. Aliens' skin is covered with small pores that have multiple functions and purposes we do not fully understand.

11. At the dawn of humanity, several human species had long tail. And the modern human beings were genetically created by the Anunnaki.

135

12. An archaic human-reptilian race lived on planet Earth.

13. Meteors or other celestial bodies did not kill the dinosaurs. It never happened.

14. At one time, the Anunnaki had settlements on the Moon and Mars.

15. The hybrid race is genetically created by the intraterrestrials.

16. There are 4 hybrid generations and three types. One of these generations lives among us.

17. The human race is not important to aliens.

18. Earth is the dumpster of the universe we know.

19. There is no reincarnation. However dead people trapped in the doomed zone (Marash Mawta) can re-appear and re-manifest themselves physically and holographically.

20. Ghosts are the projection of a time-space imprints. They are their own imprints, produced by time-space memory.

21. God was invented by the early human beings.
This item for reasons I don't understand was mentioned twice in the Transcripts.

22. There is no hell and there is no heaven in the afterlife.

23. The Exodus never happened.

24. Jesus Christ did not die on the Cross.

25. Jesus Christ was not born in Israel, but in Egypt.
(Note: Ironically, the Anunnaki Ulema claimed that Jesus was born in Tyre, Phoenicia.)

26. St. Joseph is not the real father of Jesus.

27. There is no soul trapped in the human body. This idea was created by the cave man even though he did not understand what soul is. It was his way to communicate with the "Divine" and the supernatural. The early Hittites knew this.
And The Anunnaki Ulema told us about the concept of soul in their Kira'at.

28. Civilization was not created by the Mesopotamians. It was exported to their lands by the Anatolians (Plateau of Turkey), and the early inhabitants of Phoenicia, at a time this land had no name. Later on it was called Leebaan, which means snow-white.
Civilization did not start in Mesopotamia, but first in Anatolia (Part Turkey, part ancient Armenia), continued in Phoenicia, and later on bloomed in Mesopotamia.

This item was mentioned twice in the Transcripts.

29. Turkey and the Anatolian Plateau gave birth to the first form of civilization on Earth.

30. The universe was created from within; an implosion on the inside and collisions of bubbles on the outside.

This item for reasons I don't understand was mentioned twice in the Transcripts.

31. There are multiple dimensions beyond our physical world. And within each layer of dimension, there is a multitude of other forms of dimensions.

32. There are copies of us in other dimensions.

33. Planet Earth will cease to exist in 5 billion years, along with the Moon.

34. There are "artificial" settlements and tunnels inside the Moon.

35. Many regions inside the Moon are filled with life-forms.

36. The Grays saved planet Earth from annihilation when they redirect the trajectory of a huge celestial body heading toward Earth. This happened already twice.

37. The Pyramids are 10,900-11,000 year old. And were not built by the Egyptians or any human race. The stones were teleported. This item for reasons I don't understand was mentioned twice in the Transcripts.

38. Earth ax shifted 4 times before.

39. Dark matter is what keeps the universe in place and in order, and contributes to its expansion.

This item for reasons I don't understand was mentioned twice in the Transcripts.

40. The shortest distance between A and B is not a straight line, but a bent trajectory between two dots on a parallel plane.

41. The universe bends on itself.

42. At the very beginning, Earth had the shape of an egg. It was never totally round.

43. The United States is the only country on Earth which has at its disposal a "Vortex Tunnel Weapon System". The aliens called it the "Vacuum Continuum Path" (VCP).

44. A former President of the United States Okayed operations to uncover and investigate anything and everything related to aliens' existence on Earth.

He informed an intelligence agency to gather everything they could find, here and abroad and create a file (Dossier). And the President specifically informed the agency that he is NOT interested in reading their reports and learning about their findings.

The Pyramids of Giza.

The aliens told us that the Pyramids are 10,900-11,000 year old. The foundation of the early ones were submerged by a huge regional flood in the desert some 11,000 years ago. The flood inundation traces, marks and imprints are still visible.
They were not built by the Egyptians or by any human race.

The stones were teleported and lifted up in the air like feathers, without the use of traditional cranes and winches. How? Nobody really knows. But the Anunnaki Ulema do, and I have written on the subject in a book I wrote about Baalbeck.

Egyptian inscriptions on the interior walls of the Pyramids were engraved thousands of years later by Egyptian and Nubian workers and masons.Note: According to the account of a credible contactee, the Grays told him, the Pyramids were built 10,300 years ago.

He gave the agency carte blanche, with unlimited authority and power. He also authorized the agency to solicit the help of foreign agents, if necessary.

The agency did.

Russian operatives and British agents worked for the agency.

The agency recruited four former British code breakers, who cracked the code of the German Enigma Machine at the signals intelligence center at Bletchley Park in England.

In fact, two scientists from Poland were the first to unlock the complicated mechanism of Enigma, and decipher its codes, not the Brits.

Alan Turing, was one of the first British code breakers who joined the agency efforts to learn more about aliens symbols and codes.

On more than one occasion, the President told the head of the agency not to bother him anymore with UFO and aliens stuff.

And he made it clear to him, that nobody, no other agency, no one, not even the Air Force should know about this. In other words and simply put, they had to report to nobody, no one!

Director of the FBI, Edgar J. Hoover and the military found out and were pissed off.

Later on, when the Pentagon and Air Force became heavily involved with UFOs, and took over the whole thing, Hoover wrote to them and asked to be permanently informed.

In one of his letters he precisely showed an interest in the recovered dead bodies of three aliens.

The military ignored his request, and he went berserk.
But somehow, Hoover got some very important documents from
the intelligence agency.

The Enigma machine.

President Truman and President Eisenhower were the only two
American Presidents who were vividly interested in the aliens'
question; they took a vital part and played a major role in creating
a protocol and procedures on how to initiate and conduct
investigations, and gather information. Both presidents allocated
huge secret budgets for aliens' studies and UFOs research.

140

Along with President George Bush, Sr., at the time he was the director of the CIA, Eisenhower and Truman are considered to be the most knowledgeable high officials on matters related to aliens, the Grays in particular, and UFOs.

Eisenhower remained extremely interested in aliens, UFOs and extraterrestrial technology, and how it could be used militarily. President Truman by the end of his presidency lost interest in UFOs and aliens, who once called "Space Monkeys"!

45. One committee was created to oversee the whole "progress". It was headed by a 2 star general.

Members of the committee:

- Three distinguished scientists,
- A linguist,
- Two code breakers, one from the United States, the other from Great Britain,
- A cryptology expert, in a different capacity than the code breakers/decipherers,
- A pathologist,
- A Lt. Colonel, transferred either from the Pentagon or the Air force,
- A high-ranking official from an intelligence agency,
- An expert photographer,
- A Captain,
- A typist,
- A civilian whose identity was only known to the 2 star general.

A few months later, the panel got bigger and bigger, to include:

- A- An admiral,
- b- An astronomer,
- c- A test-pilot from the Air Force,
- d- A nuclear physicist who worked at Los Alamos,
- e- A noted German scientist,
- f- A highly regarded university professor,
- g- A geologist/botanist who never said a word.

This is not the MJ-12 legendary panel, which is unfortunately to ufology and ufologists an elaborate scheme, created by three gentlemen, and regrettably swallowed by an avalanche of honest but ill-informed authors. They were simply duped!! C'est la vie!

Alan Turing

Bletchley Park in England; the UK code breaking center, where Alan Turing worked during and after Word War Two.

The house of Alan Turing, called the "Cottage", located near the main carriage house and the Bletchley Mansion.

Huts, 3, 6 and 1, where cryptology was conducted. After WWII, they were abandoned. Top code breakers who worked in these huts began a new career totally unrelated to war efforts: Aliens and aliens' technology!

46. In the early fifties, a UFO crashed in Mexico, and human bodies' parts were found inside the craft.

When the military confronted the Grays, they were shocked to hear the Grays telling them that the UFO was not one of theirs.

Furthermore, they explained to the military that not all UFOs come from the same origin.

They pointed out that the crescent-shape UFOs were piloted by another race which from time to time enters our space. And there is nothing we can do about it.

145

When a general asked if THEY (Grays) could do something about it, the aliens said NO, because those spacecrafts are in fact time machines, difficult to spot, pursue and chase.

In the Transcripts, this incident was revisited twice, and marked in 3 footnotes.

Many years later, when another intelligence/security agency was created, the incident was brought up, and dissected piece by piece. It was concluded that in fact, the Grays were no part of it, and the bodies parts were those of native Mexicans from the Aztec's region, not Americans. For a while they rested their case.

However, three years later, upon the request of a retired general who became a very influential politician/lawmaker, the case was reopened and re-examined.

The conclusions were horrifying, and I am not in liberty to reveal any information about the investigation. But bear in mind, and never forget this: The United States Air Force, the CIA and the other intelligence agency were not aware of what the aliens were doing at that time.

It was only in mid 1960, they became fully aware of what was going on, and they adopted a new policy and protocol in dealing with aliens. And this was done against all odds, and by taking huge risks, for aliens are millions of years a head of us on all levels, especially technology, science and warfare.

Some sort of agreement was discussed to prevent further atrocities. And to a great degree, it was successful.

And the Transcripts show that the UFO's crash in Mexico was totally unrelated to other alleged or assumed UFOs' crashes in the United States, for they were piloted by a different alien race.

This crash was never mentioned in Grudge, the Blue Book, the Condon Report, or in any official report on UFOs.

Bear in mind that very sensitive situations/cases, embarrassing sightings, possible UFOs' crashes and/or landings with "military implications", and confrontations with non-human entities (Aliens of any classification) were never mentioned in any official report on UFOs, and were never brought to the attention of civilian scientists (Astronomers and astrophysicists) who were hired by the government, by order from the "Big Boss".

146

47. Some UFOs reactors (engines) used water as fuel, and no scientist on Earth could understand how these reactors function. The reactors were very small, impeccably clean, and without any "trace of combustion."

48. Not all aliens are called aliens by the military.

There is an extensive catalogue listing and describing all the non-human beings and entities (known to the military and to two intelligence/security agencies), who either have entered in direct contact with us, or were described to us by aliens we have worked with.

For example, the intraterrestrials who originally came from Zeta Reticuli, millions of years ago told us that not all aliens look alike. Some don't have eyes, others don't have ears, and a great number of them don't have hands, lungs and body organs similar to ours.

For on their planets, ears, eyes, hands and lungs are useless.

They even gave us the names of multiple aliens' species and races from our galaxy and beyond.

49. Early reports on a UFO crash near Roswell indicate that 3 aliens were dead and their bodies were recovered. The fourth one was found alive but disoriented. He/she/it was approximately five foot tall; a second report indicates that the surviving alien was four foot tall. In the original (First report) report which also contained "medical observations", it was noted that the surviving alien has no gender.

Later on, in a communiqué sent to the Pentagon, the surviving alien's gender was acknowledged as a male; however no genital organs were visible.

The story is getting more complicated, because rumors start to circulate that the alien was a female indeed, because herself told them about her gender. I tend to believe that the surviving alien was de facto a female; a hybrid-female, not totally Gray.

Following an autopsy conducted on the aliens' dead bodies, the two medical examiners came to an astonishing conclusion:

- a-The aliens had no lungs.
- b-The aliens had no digestive system.
- c-The aliens had a green color blood.

147

- d-The aliens had no retina.
- e-The aliens had no genitals. This item was mentioned twice in the Transcripts
- f-The aliens had no vocal chords.
- g-The aliens were very sensitive to light.
- h-The aliens had three fingers.
- i-The aliens could not move their heads, up and down, right and left without turning their whole body.
- g-The size of their brains was extremely large *par rapport* to the size of their skull.
- h-The aliens suits were "glued" to their bodies, as if the suits were part of their skin. And much more.

A military scientist later added, that there were two different kinds of very thin metallic bands the aliens attached to their heads, and but could not figure out how they worked or for what purposes.
Three years later, another scientist found out that those bands were used by the aliens for communication and navigation, and claimed that UFOs were piloted by the mind power of the aliens. Meaning the thoughts of the aliens guided the spacecrafts.
50. The Anunnaki, Igigi, and Lyrans created and upgraded several models/specimens, prototypes and species of early quasi human and human beings. The following refers to these species:
• Ilda
• Izraelim
• Lilith, Adam, and Eve. Clergymen who attended the early meetings refuted any information and comments on this.
• Adama
• Adamu
• Adapa
• Akama-r
• Akamu "Akama"
• Alu
• Bashar
• The Space-made human creatures
• The oceans-made human creatures
• Behemoth

- Ezakarerdi, "E-zakar-erdi "Azakar.Ki"
- Ezakarfalki "E-zakar-falki"
- Ezbahaiim-erdi
- Ezeridim
- Ezrai-il "Izra'il"
- Anafar Jin Markah
- Fari-narif "Fari-Hanif"
- Gaffarim
- Negative entities, reptilians, and intelligent life-forms which live in the lower sphere/zone (Alternate dimension), and on Earth. Anthropologists who attended the earliest meetings established an elaborate chart on this category.

Galas

Ghool "Ghul"

Hay-yah

- Helama-Gooliim
- Djinn, Jinn. A famous scientist, and a university professor who worked on two major space expeditions, and closely interacted with astronauts provided his expertise on the subject of Djinn, considering the fact, that he came from a country, where an extensive literature, and an abundance of lore, myths, beliefs and stories materials were accessible to him.

- Afa-rit
- Zalmat Gaguadi, "Zalmat Shawdah"
- Zakar
- Zamzummim
- The "Women of the Light"
- Abd
- Abel "Abhal", "A-bel-alu", "Abhel", "Ablu", "Habeel"
- Abkalu "Apkallu"
- Siddim
- Dingir
- Dybukur
- Gab'r (Ga'br)
- Gabra'il "Gabriel
- Hawwah
- Lilith

• Malak
• Rephaim "Rpum"
• Lulu
•Nafari "Nafarim"

Military scientists and "model makers" attempted to forensically recreate full-size specimens of early human and quasi-human races/species based upon direct instructions and anatomical descriptions given by the intraterrestrials. First, they contacted the curator of a famous institution-museum in Washington, D.C., the curator candidly told them that it couldn't be done.
He suggested that they contact a noted Hollywood's director-producer known for using fantastic special effects and robotics. The Hollywood's man recommended a few artists who work at Walt Disney's studio. The people at Disney began to work on the project, which in its second phase ended in the laboratory/atelier of one of the major universities in Israel.
Anti-Semite whistleblowers and snitches complained, and rushed to conclude that it was a Jewish conspiracy!
It is absolutely ridiculous! Finally, after 4 years of creative and pioneering work, some archaic humans and quasi-human forms (Mannequins) came to life, and an extensive cataloging process began.
According to the intraterrestrials' account, some of the early humans, more correctly quasi-humans had a long tail, and co-habited with other reptilian races and Afrits a large area in ancient Turkey.
Some were captured by travelers from outer space, such as the Anunnaki and Igigi. It was very clear from the Grays' narrative description of the Anunnaki and their genetic programs, that they hated the Anunnaki and their offspring. This subject was not an interesting topic to military, but the anthropologists who were present at the early meetings, convinced the military that such information is priceless, because it could explain the origin of Man, and our place in the universe. So, the subject was kept wide open, and many questions were asked. At one point during the discussion, the Grays told us that a visit to Cappadocia in Turkey could be very useful, informative and convincing.

They also suggested to the military to visit Derinkuyu and Gobekli Tepe. The generals were not impressed. It took the military almost sixty years to show a serious interest in anthropology and the ancient history of humanity; military archeological excavations and diggings began during the United States invasion of Iraq.

And uncovered cuneiform writings on cylinder seals and slabs were sent to scholars and linguists in the United States to decipher them, translate them, and find out if they could shed valuable information that could be used militarily!!

51. The Anunnaki attacked the intraterrestrials (The Grays) in Sodom and Gomorrah.

52. The Grays were not happy about the military holding in custody one of their pilots; the one we captured, after their spacecraft crashed near Roswell.

53. The Grays asked the military to retrieve the dead bodies of three of their own who died after their spacecraft crashed near Roswell. Unfortunately it was too late, because the corpses were sent to a military base, and ended on the autopsy tables at Walter Reed Hospital in Maryland, USA.

54. The Grays have a time-space memory calendar that records all the events that occurred on Earth.

55. The Anunnaki taught a human race which lived in Phoenicia and Turkey, how to talk and use an intelligent language, some 9,000 years ago.

56. There are copies of each one of us in different dimensions. This item was mentioned twice in the Transcripts.

57. There are multiple dimensions in the universe, such as:
- a- Parallel dimension,
- b- Ultra dimension,
- c- Adjacent zone,
- d- Etheric zone,
- e- Future's dimension,
- f- Plasmic zone,
- g- Time dimension,
- h-And there are 12 interconnected dimensions that are constantly expanding.

These zones and dimensions vary from one galaxy to another.

58. Black holes as well as white holes contain dark energy, white energy, dark matter, and neutral matter, gravity and anti-gravity, and time-space memory.

59. The universe-space has its own memory. It transcends space itself and time.

60. Their spacecrafts are made from several components; the most important one is "Metal Memory".

61. In some dimensions, future does not exist, and in some other dimension, the past is not created yet.

62. Our universe is one of many in the 'multiverse'. And the multiuniverse bends on itself and bumps into its multi-layers, thus constantly creating more universes, including galaxies, and black holes. This item was mentioned twice in the Transcript and had 2 separate footnotes.

63. Einstein's general theory of relativity is not totally correct. It is only applicable to space-zones where our laws of physics are equally applicable.

64. The universe expands in multiple directions, through the "dark energy flow". And if the universe ceases to exist, copies of the extinct universe will re-animate a new beginning that will explode into billions of new universes.

65. At one point in the universe, some galaxies were flat. And in the dark space of these galaxies, other time-spaces universes are constantly created.

66. Parallel universes although they are not visible to us have major effect on our psyche and eventually the future and fate of the human race.

67. Other universes leak their gravity into our world through the dilatation of "Time-Orbits" (Ba'abs). This gravity has time-space memory.

68. The big bang theory is incorrect.
The universe was created from an implosion originally rooted into the vacuum of nothingness, without time, space, past, and beginning. It exploded in the state of nothingness, thus it has no beginning and start. Implosion and collision of bubbles created billions of stars and planets. This item was mentioned before and noted twice in the Transcripts, with a minor variation.

69. We can enter a meta space-time zone, and observe what it is going to happen to planet earth, millions of years in the future, because that zone is the original picture-dimension-existence of Earth. That zone in the future is the primordial existence of planet Earth. It is the same all over the universe. Each zone is a duplicate of another; this is how the Grays explained the infinity and everlasting expansion of the universe.

70. The Grays told the military how to get to the Moon in minutes, using "Route Orbital X", as called in the Transcripts. This route is accessible once every 25 years from Earth, and 7 years from Mars, unless they use the Ba'ab.

71. There are several Ba'abs around planet Earth. These are the gates to parallel universes. New York and Chicago have several Ba'abs.

72. Although there is no wind on the Moon, it could be created from dark energy and channeled to the Moon.

73. The Anunnaki built stations on the Moon and Mars before they landed on Earth.

74. The Anunnaki created us as humanoid-robots to serve their needs. We were "re-transformed" into humans following years of genetic manipulations.

This item was mentioned twice in the Transcripts.

75. None of the galactic civilizations is interested in us.

And if for some reasons, outer of space travelers land on earth, this would/could be a bad day for the human race.

Only aquatic creatures' lives would be sparred.

This item was mentioned twice in the Transcripts.

76. It is not advisable to communicate with other civilizations, because our messages appear to them as "signs of disturbance".

77. To entities on other planets and multi-dimensional zones, eyes like ours are not needed, for they use different organs to see; some use skins pores, others cells in the brain. And the brain is not necessary located inside a skull; it could be found anywhere under the skin, or on the surface.

78. Humans have more than one brain in one location, although it is invisible to the naked eye.

79. Very advanced communities live underwater and inside the Earth.

They know who we are, what we do, and how long we have been living on the surface of the Earth. Some emerged in the past to teach early humans the art of speaking, writing and fishing.

The Anunnaki created the Euphrates and Tiger Rivers. And for a long time could not control their flow. This led to periodic floods; one of them is the great regional deluge in the Middle East.

80. It is the vibrational projection of the cells in the human brain that lasts after death and is retransformed into another form of energy, not what we call the "Soul". Because soul as we think we know it does not exist; it is an idea created by early human beings for reasons not worthy discussing. The Anunnaki Ulema said the very same thing.

81. Human beings are the only race in the universe they know, which uses sex to reproduce.

82. Human beings are the only race in the universe they know, which has waste inside the body.

83. The continent of Mu existed at one time in history, but was de-fragmented and dispersed over multiple areas of the planet.

84. On other planets in our galaxy and beyond, and particularly in multi-dimensional zones or time-space zones, past, present and future concurrently exist on the same plane. This multi-co-existences allow other species to navigate time back and forth in no-time.

85. The intraterrestrials have no territorial ambitions, for they could not survive on the surface of Earth for a long period. Their body's composition and structure would not allow them to survive for long time. The oxygen we breathe is poison to them. This item was mentioned twice in the Transcripts.

86. Neither the theory of Evolution nor the theory of the Creation is correct.

Only a genetic manipulation of DNA sequences created the modern physiognomy of the human race, and stayed the very same for the past 11,000 years. The early form of humans was created some 65,000 years ago.

87. All civilizations in our galaxy are highly advanced, and none of them has any interest in communicating with us.

88. The nearest advanced civilization to Earth is 10^5 light years.

89. From an anthropologist and military scientist: The Grays purposely rewind time, past and future, to convince their abductees of their powers and intent to create a better world.

They Grays have no sense of time.

However, they can clearly differentiate between past events and future events. They do not follow any chonological order or time-frame sequences when they project holographic images. Are they deliberately confusing their abductees? I don't think so.

90. Quite often, abductees are confused by the variety and speed of images they see on a holographic screen. It is not always the message, but the intent of the Grays that confuses them.

My personal opinion: It is not in the best interest of the Grays to confuse the abductees. The Grays have no intent to confuse the abductees, simply because, the abductees were already confused by the whole experience. Anybody would be confused, if he/she has been subjected to such an extraordinary incident.

The confusion usually begins, as soon as the apparition of aliens occurs; long before, the Grays lift up, levitate, and abduct people.

Most certainly, more confusions will follow up, when:
- a-The abductees enter a spaceship out of this world,
- b-The abductees are shown holographic images and footages;
- c-Are directed to an operating room,
- d-The aliens place them on a surgical bed,
- e-The abductees see strange aliens operating on them;
- f-The aliens show them the "Little Black Box".
- g-Etc., etc.

All these sequences, events, and related phases of the abduction confuse the abductees. It is not exclusively the message or the speech of the aliens that confuse the abductees, but the whole process.

91. The Grays have at their disposal all the mental, intellectual, scientific, paranormal, and physical means and tools to paralyze, handicap, incapacitate, and control the physical, mental, emotional, and psychological faculties of the abductees.

92. To assume that the intraterrestrials (The Alien Grays) are not worried about continuous underground atomic/nuclear tests and detonations is absurd. Although, each meeting focused on several issues, the question of atomic/nuclear arsenal, and underground detonations was of a major concern to the aliens.

93. The Grays do not give a damn about our forests and the purity of our environment; water, air and Earth's ecology. They do not breathe our air...nor do they drink our water. They are afraid that what we are doing could blow up the whole damned Earth.

They live here. the Grays have established their habitat on Earth, millions of years ago, long before man walked on the surface of the globe. It is quite reasonable to conclude that the Grays are seriously concerned about Earth's safety, simply because they share it with us. Earth's environment should be understood as the safety of planet Earth, and continuity of life on the surface of Earth and beneath (Underground).

94. In 1992, the Grays met twice with civilian delegates, scientists and military men (Two Generals and one Lt. Colonel), in Arizona and Alaska. And they reached a final agreement, and a complete understanding that all underground testings should cease immediately.

As a result, the United States stopped undergound nuclear testings in 1992. Other leading countries followed suit.

England's last nuclear testing occurred in 1991, Russia in 1990.

France and China had a surprise-visit by the Grays in 1996. And before the end of 1996, both France and China abandonned their nuclear testings. In 1998, Pakistan and India were confronted by angry Grays, when both country detonnated their atomic bombs in the same year. The Pakistani and Indians got the message of the Grays.

95. In modern times, zooming into the past did occur accidentally, during one of the phases of Project Serpo. The original Serpo team consisted of ten members – nine men and one woman.

The woman was released from the team project when the military found out that she was pregnant, thus only the nine men went through the Stargate initially. They zoomed into the future, into the realm of three star systems outside of our galaxy.

156

The plan was to have traveled to the Grays' Zeta Reticuli, but the stargate sent them somewhere else, for unknown reasons.

The data entered to go through the stargate, had included seven planets that had atmospheres and climates similar to that of Planet Earth. The ship these men traveled in through the stargate was made for that trip by the Zeta Reticulan Grays.

Unfortunately, they did not end up in the Zeta Reticulan star system, and while stuck there, ran out of food and supplies, causing the death of three of the men.

This catastrophic mistake could have easily been avoided, had one of the pilots been a Zeta Reticulan, as was suggested by the Zeta Reticulan Grays.

The military refused since they did not fully trust the aliens, and decided to go only with the two human pilots, that had been trained on Gray ships for a period of just twelve months, on a secret base in Alaska.

The reason for taking the pregnant woman off the team, was due to the fact that had she given birth in another planetary system, and in another time/dimension, her son would return far older than his mother (perhaps by a hundred thousand years) and military scientists were not yet ready to deal with such situations. The reasons for this being that her baby's birth in another system, under different conditions/were born on Earth.

There was no contact between Earth and the crew for three Earth years. A military scientist was told by one of the Grays that it had taken them (The Grays) only ten minutes to get there.

Upon the return of the surviving six team members, and before the project was completely abandoned, Carl Sagan suggested another attempt be made to go to the Zeta Reticulan system, this time using one of the Gray pilots, in a second ship that had been built for this mission, with three other members added onto Project Serpo.

For the record, the Zeta Reticulan pilot's name was Ramu.

Again, they went through the stargate, but this time were zoomed back in time and space here on Earth and into another dimension.

157

It was at this point that Carl Sagan pointed out to the military, how this technology could be used against the human race, by the Zeta Reticulan Grays, having realized that both expeditions into the past and future were deliberate diversions on the part of the aliens.

96. In 1957 and 1958, the Gray aliens told President Eisenhower about the rewinding of time technology. The military scientists and President Eisenhower did not believe it is possible, until the Grays "rewound the tape of time" to the point where they were able to not only see a holographic projection of Jesus, but listen to his voice as well.

General Marshall was present at this meeting, and decided to ask the Grays if they could re-project an event that occurred in World War II, known only to General Omar Bradley, General Patton, General Eisenhower and himself.

He gave them the date and location of this event, and waited for the holographic projection. What they then saw before them, was accurate down to the very last detail. The Grays then went even one step further to reveal two letters within the holographic projection:

One, was a speech to be given by Eisenhower in the event of a successful storming of the beaches of Normandy on D-Day, and another speech to be given, in the event that this D-Day event was a failure. The existence and contents of the two letters were known only to General Bradley and Eisenhower. Also shown were the six draft letters written by Eisenhower and his secretary.

97. The "Alien Black Box": It is a little black box, the alien abductors, (in some unspecified instances) show to abductees, point to it, and return to their spacecraft. The little black box contains a live fetus of a hybrid entity (creature), which is part human and part alien Gray.

The aliens show the Black Box to their abductees, and point them to a small entity which resembles human beings; sometime, they are babies, and some other time, adult (Males and females). The aliens don't say a word. They just open the box and display its content. The intention of the aliens is clear: Look and see how we can duplicate you and create your replacement!

What the abductees see is essentially a holographic photo of their children; children they will give birth to, when impregnated artificially in the aliens' test-tubes.

98. BCB: Acronym for the Black Conic Box, also known as the "Compressor". Insiders and scientists nickname the program, the "gadget" the "Compressor". The gadget consists of a small black cylindrical container, 1 foot in height by ½ foot in width. It is a movable (Mobile) device that functions without an external source of energy. In other words, it works without an electric current, batteries, or any similar source of power. It is neither electronic nor atomic.

It is programmable and re-programmable. It draws its energy from within. An internal cell located in the very inner circle of the cone emits an enormous amount of "sucking power" capable of absorbing, transporting, resizing, and condensing a large amount of contents and materials into the cone.

The 'sucked up' materials can be anything, all sorts of things...the box can suck up everything you have in your apartment, absolutely everything, chairs, tables, furniture, your bed, your closets, your clothes and even your pets, melt them like ice-cream and boom, shoot them right in the box.

The "Sucking Power" of this device has the capability of de-fragmenting any object, and reducing it to any desirable size, density, format and weight.

This is based upon the fact, that everything in the universe is made out of molecules, and the density of the molecules dictates the nature, weight and size of any object, any substance, any matter in the world.

By reducing, decreasing, increasing and/or altering the properties of molecules, any object can be reduced and/or enlarged either to the biggest or smallest desired shape, and consequently be transported to any destination, regardless of space, distance, and time. The process can also de-fragment the molecules to a certain point, where the biggest object can fit inside the smallest possible container.

The BCB can destroy or confuse a person's ATP (Adenosine Triphosphate), which is the energy coin of the cell.

When cells are destroyed, molecules and membranes die.

The "Sucking Machine" de-regulates the transfer of energy and all sources of vitality from chemical bonds to your body absorbing energy called Endergonic, and causes destructive reactions in the cell.

The BCB can also be used as a "mental weapon". It controls everything in your mind and in your body. It creates new habits, and makes you addicted to "something you don't want in your life". Because it empties your brain from all its contents, and put in (in your brain) new things, new information, new habits, new desires and new thoughts, the person who is operating the machine becomes your master.

99. The Neutron Bomb: Also called an "Enhanced Radiation Weapon", the ERW or Neutron bomb is a type of thermonuclear weapon.

An ERW is any weapon used to magnify radiation production, beyond what is normal for an atomic device. The research on this weapon system, was started in 1956, reached its peak in 1958, and is generally credited to Samuel Cohen (the self-proclaimed neurotic), of the Lawrence Livermore Laboratory, who was a protégé of Edward Teller – the father of the Hydrogen Bomb. The purpose of this weapon is to destroy every living biological life form, without destroying infrastructure.

Every human and living thing will die, and the area can be captured, taken over and moved into after about a month.

The Neutron bomb is a tactical weapon, developed specifically to release a very large portion of its energy, as highly energetic nuclear radiation, to harm biological tissues without causing nuclear fallout.

Two types of the Neutron Bomb: The AGM-114N, also referred to as the "Plastic Neutron Bomb". It causes this most excruciating and painful death, because it releases a massive amounts of free neutrons, and breaks down the molecular structures of all living biological things, that basically hemorrhage to death.

Unlike heavy elements such as caesium, uranium and plutonium that cause nuclear fallout and have very long half-lives, neutron particles will be absorbed in a very short time, rendering no lasting damage to subsequent life forms after a period of a month or so.

The Neutron Bombs were intended to deliver a dose of 80Gy, to produce immediate and permanent incapacitation.

However, one significant drawback of this weapon is that not all targeted troops will die, or be incapacitated immediately. From ground zero and up to 1,000 yards away, most every living thing will be totally incapacitated within minutes, and physiologically will become the most miserable creature imaginable, with blood exploding out of every orifice in its body.

Further out than 1,000 yards, many of those hit will experience a brief bout of nausea, followed by a temporary recovery, known as the "walking ghost" phase, lasting days to weeks. These victims will be aware of their inevitable fate, having witnessed those who had died the most agonizing death imaginable.

Neutron bombs are expensive to make and maintain, due to the relatively short half-life of Tritium (12.3 yrs). The Neutron-Oxygen bomb (according to the blueprints provided by the Grays), does not produce any explosion, heat, fire or sound, or any infrastructural damage.

It specifically targets the brain and respiratory system. Once it is dropped, every living thing that requires oxygen to breathe will be asphyxiated. The data on the volume of air, and extent of the atmosphere affected by this bomb, is still being kept top secret. However an experiment to this effect was conducted on a remote island in the Pacific Ocean in the late 1950's.

A small airport facility was built, with perishables and livestock placed on the island. After the bomb was dropped from the aircraft, the pilot said he observed what appeared to be an umbrella looking that momentarily opened and then closed back down on itself.

No smoke, no fire and no sound were seen or heard from the detonation of this bomb.

Other military saw it differently, describing it as if it looked like a large fishing net being thrown over an area into the water, then disappearing. To date, this weapon has not been used on any human civilian population, or military troops in any country.

100. Hybrids' three distinct groups/categories: The first group is born from the first combination of abductees' and Grays' DNA. They closely resemble the Grays.

The second group is the middle-stage hybrids; they are the result of mating between these early-stage ones. Middle-stage hybrids are mated with humans to create them – and they can hardly be distinguished from humans.

The third group is the late-stage hybrid, known as the human-hybrids. They look exactly like human beings, but are much shorter, and have different facial structure. The hybrid children (from 2 years to 5 years) live in two different ways: a) Human environment, and b) underground/underwater communities.

It is a large communal living in underground and/or underwater dormitories, or sometimes in above ground level dormitories, but always on Earth.

101. Since time is not linear, aliens can travel "Jump" into the future, and revisit the past simultaneously. Intraterrestrials and extraterrestrials don't need special spacecrafts to do that.

102. There is a total of 4 UFOs crashes on record; three in the United States, and one in Mexico. Two aliens who survived the crash were retained by the government.

The others were found dead, assumingly on impact.

From the two surviving aliens, one died after a few months; the other remained on the American soil for 6 months.

Using a device created by both aliens (Separately, in each case), we were able to communicate three times with an intraterrestial community living on Earth. The devise was confiscated by our scientists who tried unsuccessfully to unlock the secrets of its mechanism.

The devise stopped to work when the first alien passed away, and the second one stopped to send and receive messages, when a military science passed it under an X ray machine.

103. Although the aliens' spacecrafts were severely damaged, we were able to retrieve gadgets and tools from the interior of the crafts which were intact. A reverse engineering program began to find out how these tools functioned, but all efforts were useless.

162

In addition to a whole team of military scientists from the Air Force and Navy, three eminent civilian engineers working at a major research and development laboratory were contracted by the government. Years later, one of those civilian engineers was credited with the discovery of...which has changed our way of life, and understanding of science and optics.

104. The words UFOs were never used in the meetings and in writing the Transcripts. The word "Disc", and sometimes "Disk" were used instead.

105. Alpha team consisted of military officers and the nation's best scientists. It was under the control of the Air Force and the Navy. Three months later, an intelligence agency took over, and the military's role was reduced to supplying pilots and personnel.

106. A web of 17 underwater channels linked the aliens to their habitats, headquarters and communities. Starting in 1997, the web will be referred to as the "Net", and the channels will be called "Tubes".

107. Aquatic Plasma Corridors: The Russians have a massive underwater base that was created in 1969, to study an extraterrestrial underwater navigation system called the "Aquatic Plasma Corridors".

This corridor is undetectable by satellite, sonar or any other underwater detection system. Not all branches of the Russian Navy were aware of the creation/existence of this base.

During one of their naval maneuvers just outside the perimeter of this Russian underwater base, six frogmen from one of the Russian submarines encountered three alien frogmen in metallic suits underneath a massive metallic object.

Both the Russian and alien frogmen were roughly at a depth of one hundred to one hundred and twenty feet.

The alien frogmen were wearing what appeared underwater to be metallic suits of indeterminable and interchanging colors that morphed from a silvery white to bluish to grey.

One of the Russian frogmen stated that when he tried to approach these three, he was blocked by what seemed to be an invisible underwater force-field, created by the alien frogmen as a protection shield.

The Russian frogman's oxygen tanks started to fail and he quickly lost consciousness and started sinking but was saved by one of his fellow divers. After being rescued, he described the alien frogmen as being 8ft to 11ft tall, as he saw them underwater. And none of them had any visible oxygen tanks/breathing apparatus attached to them.

In the secret debriefing that followed, the Russian diver who saved his fellow frogmen, said that when he too tried to approach this massive foreign submerged object, he encountered what felt like a solid transparent wall surrounding the object. He later described it as an oval glass box, surrounding this mysterious submerged object which also shielded it from contact with the ocean's water.

After the fall of the Berlin wall, and ensuing collapse of the Soviet Empire, rumors started circulating within the military and scientific community, that this bizarre event was in fact a joint Russian-extraterrestrial operation designed to explore the effects of the underwater plasma corridor on it's environment in the ocean, and on humans, as well as their psychological and psychosomatic reaction to encountering the corridor and seeing the alien frogmen and the ship itself.

Two decades later in Lake Baikal, other Russian navy frogmen encountered similar 9ft "silver swimmers" who also had no visible breathing apparatus. While these encounters are largely unknown to the general public, military scientists with top clearance are well aware of them, and have worked on similar projects in different underwater bases, these massive underwater military bases, whether they be Russian, or American or Chinese, look from the surface to be rectangular/traditional compound structures.

However upon entering them underwater, they expand in all directions, and are extremely extensive. And all of them are joint human-alien operations.

Starting from the second underwater level, compartments are divided into large operation rooms, separated by elaborate long corridors, curving at 90 degrees every hundred feet or so, with doors that can drop down from the ceiling to seal off segments in the event of radiation leakage, or any matter related to internal security.

Cassini-Huygens Spacecraft.
The spacecraft captured evidence on aliens' existence and
UFOs' photos, the United States could not have access to.

One of the interesting characteristics of these doors in the
corridors is the circular porthole-like windows within what is a
whitish metal of extraterrestrial origin.
None of these metallic alloys are possible here due to earth's
gravity, and as such have to be done in orbit aboard the Space
Shuttle. Interestingly enough, this technology has been shared by
American, Russian and Israeli military scientists.

At one time British and French scientists complained of being left out of the loop, to which the Americans responded very candidly "We don't trust Europeans – especially the French!" To which the French retorted that they would withhold all information garnered from the Cassini-Huygens mission to Saturn.

An American three star general was quick to respond by saying "This is not the first time you Europeans have withheld information from us. Remember the Belgian incident?" (Aurora)

The mode of transportation down to the underwater base and within the base is also fascinating.

From the surface, one enters a craft that looks like a silvery metallic spinning top, approximately 8ft in diameter, that can comfortably accommodate four passengers, and corkscrews its way downwards centrifugally around a rod using a form of magnetic propulsion for what seems to be a only a few seconds down to an unknown depth.

From the second underwater level on down, the "Spinning Mobile Satellite" (SMS) travels horizontally and reaches its final destination at an undisclosed level of the base at which it again dives into water. It is at that level/destination that you will find the habitat and work center of the Grays.

108. The Vortex Tunnel: Created by a group of daring avant-garde scientists, who obtained a government contract to develop this most unusual weapon. It is sometimes jokingly referred to as "the straw".

The vortex tunnel can be turned on and turned off at will, and is a project that was started in the 1960's and became fully operational in the 1970's. When activated (usually done in open fields in the American mid-west, away from farming and populated areas), an invisible vortex opening that is about ten feet wide, sucks in everything in its path, up to 500 feet in all directions.

This is only one of its functions. Its primary purpose is to do just the opposite – but to propel object and people into an opening created by its operation that leads into another dimension very close to the one we live in.

The military has successfully sent some of its military personnel who volunteered for the experiment and were sent through a vortex tunnel to this other dimension and brought back.

Within close circles it is also referred to as the "TTT" or the "Tag Team Tunnel". This team of six were sent through the vortex and were supposed to have returned within a matter of ten to fifteen seconds, but ended up gone for fifteen minutes.

When they asked the Gray personnel working with them on this project why the men had not immediately returned, the Gray scientist laughed at them. At which point they demanded he goes through the tunnel himself to retrieve the men.

Within a few seconds, all six men and the Gray were back.

In the debriefing that followed, the six volunteers said that the dimension they were in was so close to ours, as to be able to see and hear one Major put a gun to the head of the Gray, saying "You better go in there right now buddy and get my men back!" The Gray laughed at him but returned with the six.

Apparently all Gray aliens are known to play tricks and games like these with the military, within many of these joint projects.

What did the men see, hear and feel in this other dimension so close to ours? According to the men, they saw a labyrinth of corridors before them, and the only colors they saw everything in were blue, light blue and light gray. No other colors seemed to exist in this other dimension. There was no sound or breeze or any kind of feeling in this dimension, and it felt like a void filled with corridors. The only sounds they could hear were those of the military officers and camera men behind them who were observing and filming this experiment.

Turning around to return to the room, the six volunteers said they encountered the most unusual invisible, intangible wall that would not let them come through to the physical world and dimension we live in. Try as they might, and as close as they were to the others, within inches of them in fact – and yelling and screaming to be let back in, none of the observing officers heard or saw them.

167

When the Gray went in to retrieve the six from that dimension, he had a device on his wrist that (he had withheld from the military) would be necessary for the men to return.

Upon stepping in, he grabbed a hold of the first man, and placed his other hand up to the invisible intangible wall of this dimension. The device on his wrist revealed a knob on the wall, which he turned and then told the men they could move forward. As the first man went through, to the second man standing right behind, it was as if he dematerialized to the width of a page in a book was flipped over.

The wall of this dimension now became foggy, and the other men were terrified of going through it, not knowing whether they too would be turned into sheets of paper that could be turned over as if flipping from one page to the next in a book. The Gray assured the men it was perfectly safe, and was their only back to our world, so the men had no choice but to go through.

Within the void of this dimension, there would be no food, no water, no stimuli of any kind that the human body and mind is used to.

Whoever is sent here would go insane from sensory deprivation, whilst starving to death from hunger and thirst.

109. BL-rm3: An acronym for "Blue Room Manifesto, Level 3", never used by ufologists, and/or mentioned in ufology's jargon. Many link the "Blue Room" to Wright-Patterson Air Force Base. It is not totally correct.

Simply put, the manifesto is a list/compilation of alleged aliens' artifacts, UFOs' wreckages, reports on autopsy of dead aliens' bodies, so on.

Wright-Patterson Air Force Base has long been connected to recovered UFOs, extraterrestrial debris, logs on extraterrestrial language' code, and the "storage" of dead aliens' bodies. Its Hangar 18 has been said to store the wreckage of three UFO crashes, while the "Blue Room" is believed to be the final resting place of four alien bodies. This is the first half part of its macabre enigma. The second part is its mysterious name: Blue Room!

As expected, many ufologists jumped to several conclusions which did not make sense. Some have claimed it is called blue, because the walls of the room were painted blue.

Others have suggested that "blue" means nothing in particular, at one time, and especially after the Second World War, all the interiors of military hangars, especially repair-shops were either painted blue or gray. But the truth is more colorful than blue, gray, or any other color!

A retired Lt. Colonel has leaked to close friends (Outside the military) that originally the Blue Room was not called Blue Room. In fact, it was "called nothing, at all."

He added that the room was a "small area of a huge hangar used to store military materiel. Everything changed with the arrival of bags and wooden boxes allegedly containing wreckages of an extraterrestrial spacecraft."

A retired sergeant completed the rest of the story; he said, "Bags and bags start to arrive to the Base.

Some were small and some were large, but all were black bags, you can call them body bags if you want. We had piles of them. They took a large area of the hangar. The first night, we piled them on the top of each other at one corner of the hangar.

Sometime after 3:00 am, two civilians, one colonel and one captain arrive to the hangar and started to sort out something. They were looking for something but we did not know what they were looking for. Around 7:00 am, more bags arrived, they were blue bags, I think they were 4 or five of them, I don't remember. For some reasons, more civilians arrived and were very concerned with these blue bags.

They put a tag on each one of them, and took all the bags to another area right below the hangar.

The men start to talk about these blue bags, and before you know it, everybody on the base starts to talk about the blue bags. Why these bags were special?

At the beginning nobody knew. The next day, we start to hear things, you know, things like alien crafts, alien bodies, stuff like that. I think because the blue bags were taken below, down you know, where we had iceboxes, and nobody, I mean nobody could get there, the boys start to call the room Blue Room. Yah, they called it blue room because it has the blue bags, that's all..."

According to one person who allegedly worked on a top secret alien reverse-engineering program, the storage area was called "Blue Room" because of the "many tubes and glass containers, military doctors brought to the storage room. The containers had some sort of blue liquids. And they brought lots of them."

According to one source, the blue bags were removed to another area, not Hangar 18, but to an underground bunker consisting of three levels. Level three was called the "Blue Room". Later on, level three became an "Operation Room"; a medical operation room.

Note: Worth mentioning here, that story one, story two and other allegations surrounding the blue bags and blue room were never substantiated.

110. Military bases and/or stations mentioned on more than one occasion: These bases appeared on several pages of the Transcripts for at least 3 years.

I will list them without any explanation:

- In the United States
- 1-Andrews Air Force Base
- 2-Barksdale Air Force Base
- 3-Bolling Air Force Base
- 4-Brunswick Naval Air Station
- 5-Cannon Air Force Base
- 6-Carswell Air Force Base
- 7-Edwards Air Force Base
- 8-Eglin Air Force Base
- 9-Ellington Air Force Base (a.k.a. NASA Ellington Field)
- 10-Ellsworth Air Force Base
- 11-Fairchild Air Force Base
- 12-Fort Ritchie
- 13-Grand Forks Air Force Base
- 14-Groom Lake Test Facility
- 15-Holloman Air Force Base
- 16-Homestead Air Force Base
- 17-Hunter Army Air Field
- 18-Kinchloe Air Force Base

- 19-Kinross Air Force Base
- 20-Kirtland Air Force Base
- 21-Langley Air Force Base
- 22-Loring Air Force Base
- 23-Los Alamos Research Facility
- 24-Luke Air Force Base
- 25-Malstrom Air Force Base
- 26-March Air Force Base
- 27-Maxwell Air Force Base
- 28-Minot Air Force Base
- 29-NORAD Headquarters
- 30-Norton Air Force Base
- 31-Oakdale Armory
- 32-Pease Air Force Base
- 33-The Pentagon
- 34-Peterson Air Force Base
- 35-Plattsburgh Air Force Base
- 36-Sawyer Air Force Base
- 37-Truax Air Force Base
- 38-Wright-Patterson Air Force Base
- 39-Wurtsmith Air Force Base
- Other countries
- Australia
- Pine Gap Research Facility
- Canada
- Falconbridge Air Force Station
- England
- Bentwaters Air Force Base (a.k.a. RAF Bentwaters)
- Iran
- Shahrokhi Air Force Base
- Russia
- Plesetsk Military Cosmodrome

111. Secret Projects: Also referred to as Black Operations. Some appeared once in the Transcripts, others regularly.
I will list them without any additional information.

- 1-Project Snowbird
- 2-Project Aurora
- 3-Project Excalibur
- 4-Project Blue Team
- 5-Project Sign
- 6-Project Red Light
- 7-Project Grudge/Aquarius
- 8-Project Moon Dust and Blue Fly
- 9-Project Blue Book
- 10-Project Magnet
- 11-Project Pounce/Pluto
- 12-Project Gabriel/Joshua
- 13-Project Plat
- 14-Project Luna
- 15-Project Crystal Knight
- 16-Project SERPO
- 17-TAC Star Project
- 18-D.A.R.P.A.
- 19-MK Ultra Mind Control Program

112. Grays altercations: A reference made to several altercation incidents between the military, civilian workers (Scientists, contractors, men and women) and the aliens, at underground secret bases.

A significant altercation occurred between the military and the aliens at the...laboratory. A special armed forces unit was called in to try and free a number of military personnel and scientists "trapped in the facility who had become aware of what was really going on."

Sixty six soldiers were killed in the effort, and the scientists were not freed; an agreement has been reached between the military and aliens who co-shared a secret military base, giving the aliens absolute freedom in conducting their own business in the base.

The soldiers and scientists were restricted from interfering in any activity and the...operations conducted by the alien Greys.

In addition, it was agreed upon by both parties, that the soldiers shall not bear arms in the areas under the direct control of the aliens. For some reasons, source said, "armed men entered two aliens' compartments carrying sophisticated weapons and laser-beam guns. A clash between the aliens and the military men led to several fatalities. None of the alien Greys was killed.

By 1983, the military learned about the "Aliens' Agenda" and the full scale their extensive abduction operations all over the country. Following the clash, members of the Committee... met at a country club to discuss the whole story and how to deal with the aliens.

The Country Club is a remote lodge with a private golf course, comfortable sleeping and working quarters and its own private airstrip built by and exclusively for the members of...

Some members of...who have now become military, wanted to confess the whole scheme and go public, beg their forgiveness and ask for their support.

The other part (and majority) of the Committee... argued that there was no way they could do that - that the situation was untenable and there was no use in exciting the public with the "horrible truth" and that the best plan was to continue the development of a weapon or plan of containment that could be used against the aliens under the guise of "SDI", the so-called Strategic Defense Initiative which had nothing whatsoever to do with a defense for inbound Russian nuclear missiles.

Dr. Edward Teller, "father" of the H-bomb, was seen in the nuclear test tunnels of... One insider has claimed that "Teller was driving his workers and associates like a man possessed; and well he should be for Dr. Teller is a member of the... along with Dr. ..., and Admiral...

Security guards who worked at the... ... base were regularly transferred to other units, their names and serial numbers altered.

113. Radio plasma belt (RPB) around Earth to isolate Earth from the universe: A report referred to the RPB, created by the intraterrestrials to isolate earth from the universe. This belt can expand up or down, and can affect missiles, rockets, or airplanes, and blow them up. It explains what has happened to various airplanes in Vietnam, and also to human spacecrafts and space missions.

114. The Bioelectric extraterrestrial robots "B.E.R": The topic of bioelectric robots, called also astro-biolectric robots, is not often addressed by astrobiologists, however astro-geneticists in general have shown some interest in exploring this new field of study. Only ufologists are psychologically prepared to go one step further. David Levy, an artificial-intelligence researcher at the University of Maastricht, explored the subject of robot-human intimacy in depth.

His doctoral thesis on sexbots was developed into a book titled "Love and Sex with Robots", in which he explains that "the age of robot-human unions may be closer than you think." He stated: "My forecast is that around 2050, the state of Massachusetts will be the first jurisdiction to legalize marriages with robots."

An almost similar aliens-robotics program involving humanoids-extraterrestrial robots began some years ago, under the auspices of an obscure intelligence agency, No! It is neither the CIA nor the NSA!!

Very few military scientists are aware of the existence of this program. It is Above Top Secret.

There is a most unusual project in avant-garde military-ufology referring to bioelectric extraterrestrial robots (B.E.R.) This black project program is still totally unknown to "Civilian ufologists".

BER started in September 1986 in two locations in... ...; the first, at a laboratory operated by a leading university, and the second one in an underground facility.

Essentially, BER explored the possibility of using human-like robots capable of acting like human beings.

These robots were intended to be used as replacement for the hybrids third generation, known to the public (Thanks to some colorful ufologists) as MIB (Men-in-Black).

One of the advantages of using these robots, is their EM effect on the human brain, particularly, while interacting with aliens and/or para-military's abductees, and tracking people who were used as "experimentation tools" in unauthorized mind control programs.

These robots unlike robots manufactured by companies to replace man-power tasks, move, act and communicate like human beings.

They look like us, and in many instances, they show emotion, and ordinary human reactions. The Japanese and the Chinese tried on several occasions to steal their secrets.

The effects of EM fields on areas of the brain and particularly with people who are EH (Electrically Hypersensitive) can and does cause all manner of unusual and undesirable neurological and physiological symptoms including:

- a-Visions
- b- Hallucinations
- c- Fear
- d- Anxiety
- e- Being OOB (out of body)
- f- Unconsciousness
- g- Feeling of being touched and watched
- h- Seeing UFOs
- i- Encountering aliens.

The external EM interferes with bioelectrical processes within very specific areas of the brain cortex.

BER and BER-MIB projects (Some call them programs) are not phantasmagoric ideas. They exist.

Ufologists, almost guessed what was going on, through alleged leaks, but still, they have no clues.

By pure coincidence, author and ufologist Raymond E. Fowler vaguely guessed something about these bioelectric robots, when he talked about the Watchers (The Gray entities) and called them bio-electric robots.

115. The Corridor Plasma: It was mentioned numerous times and in the meetings and recorded 4 times in the Transcripts. So, I am going to repeat what it was said.

Corridor plasma is a term used to refer to underwater tunnels and passages created and operated by aliens to navigate the oceans. By using these cold plasma tunnels, UFOs can accomplish extraordinary tasks, such as, to name a few:

- **a-** To reach an astonishing speed;
- **b-** To avoid sonar detection;
- **c-** To remain undetected by spy satellites;
- **d-** To enter and exit underwater bases.

The corridor plasma is movable and mobile, meaning that aliens can place the underwater tunnels, and displace them according to their needs, and "navigation chart".

The tunnels extend to thousands of miles underwater, and serve as a web network for several alien underwater bases around the globe. Their spaceships known as USO (Unidentified Submerged Objects) use the plasma corridors to navigate the oceans and seas. According to some, the "Corridor Plasma can be compared to a White Hole, where gravity exists no longer.

In the White Holes, the gravity as we know it becomes a reverse gravity. This phenomenon allows the alien space crafts to attain a mind-boggling speed."

Some of these bases are located in:

- **a**- The Bahamas
- **b**- The Japanese "Dragon Triangle"
- **c**- The north side of the so-called Bermuda Triangle
- **d**- Alaska
- **e**- Florida.

The Grays intraterrestrials (Aliens who live on Earth) are the inventors of this astonishing technology. He added, "One of the most amazing aspects of this technology is the fact that the aliens' underwater crafts never touch the water.

There is a plasma shield surrounding the exterior body of the craft. We know that plasma produces extreme heat. And this heat can melt the craft. But the aliens found a way to isolate the plasma heat from the body of the craft, by adding two layers of anti-plasma shields (Called Plasma Belt) to the exterior body of the craft.

116. No Presidential Executive order was ever issued to confuse the American people on matters related to UFOs and aliens.

There is an Annex/Memo which gave authority to an intelligence agency to disseminate information to confuse, disorient and misinform the Soviet Union.

In the Memo, a VERY brief reference was made to the aliens' question, recommending that UFOs and aliens matters should NOT be made public, and/or information on the subject should not be communicated to and/or shared with other agencies.

117. Although President Truman gave full authority to an intelligence agency to take care of the aliens' business, secretly he created his own committee to oversee what the agency was doing. It is very ironic, because in a previous memo, and during a verbal communication with the director of the agency, President Truman made it clear that he is NOT interested in reading the reports and findings of the agency on UFOs and aliens (Space Monkeys!) In fact, it is not so ironic, if you know a little bit about the character of President Truman.

He did it and said it on purpose, so he would and could legally and "honestly" deny any knowledge of the aliens, and UFOs. He was protecting the "integrity of the office of the President of the United States." Later, it was found out that President Truman's intention was much broader.

From left to right: President Turman, Defense Secretary James V. Forrestal

He wanted to set the foundation of isolating any politician, any senator, any congressman, including future presidents from knowing anything about UFOs and aliens.
The man did not trust anybody! His last communications with the director of the agency will occur exclusively in the Oval Office, and only Marshall was allowed to be present. Defense Secretary James V. Forrestal was barred from all meetings.

On May 22, 1949, the ousted Forrestal committed suicide at the Bethesda Naval Hospital, Maryland, USA. He was "quarantined" on the 16th floor suite, for psychiatric evaluation and care. Report on his death as issued by the hospital stated that he jumped from a window in the 16th floor hall. A very close associate of his said, they killed him! The Secretary was taken by force to Bethesda Naval Hospital, on order from President Truman. And around the clock 4 MP were guarding his room.
A polite way to say, he was under a constant watch, not for his own safety, but to make sure that what is was "planned" will be carried out without interference and suspicion.
Many insiders believed Forrestal was the first official victim of UFOs/Aliens Cover-up.

The Transcripts did not make any reference, or referred to the suicide incident. However, insiders could not keep their mouth shot, frustrated they spread the rumors that hired operatives from... ... killed him and threw him from the window.

*** *** ***

Addendum to the Aliens' Transcripts:
Selection of subjects discussed in the meetings:

On Jesus, the 4 Bibles and Dark Matter:

One of the weirdest and unexpected things about what the aliens told an American archbishop sitting next to a famous scientist from Los Alamos laboratory at one of the early meetings with the extraterrestrials.

(The only meeting where and when a member of the clergy was invited to attend) was this: Jesus Christ did exist and made miracles; he had wisdom but he put himself into lots of troubles, really unnecessary.

We have a true account of his life that you should consider, and when we meet again we'll bring you this account, that you might call it the true bible of Jesus Christ.

The alien also said:

a-We watched Jesus, and saw him on our screens.

b-None of the four Bibles written by the disciples is in fact written by the disciples, because they were illiterate; they could not write and read, and understand ancient Greek.

Only the ruling class, the upper class of the society and highly educated people could read and speak Greek.

Jesus spoke in Aramaic, not in Hebrew. His disciples could speak only Aramaic, not even Hebrew, only Judas was fluent in Hebrew and Aramaic. There were 2 languages there. But of course Jesus knew both languages. When he argued with the Rabis he could use any of the two languages. But, his students could not.

The Hebrew was spoken few kilometers from where they use to live. And did not know a word in Hebrew. So, don't expect them to learn Greek, a language which was thousands of miles away, beside, none of them left their homeland. They were the lowest of the social class and time wise and financially could not afford to take a long trip to Greece, because they were fisherman with low income.

c-The four Bibles are not authentic.

And this is very sad for humanity because people can't distinguish between the real preacher Jesus and the mythical one they created.

More than half of each version of the four Bibles is incorrect and distorted, copied and recopied several times over, and each time new stories were added, and old ones were deleted.

That is why you see many contradictions in the Bible.

The other bibles used by the Gnostics.

The archbishop asked one of the Grays:
Question: How about the other bibles used by the Gnostics?"
The Gray's answer: Same thing, many stories were fabricated, but at least they got the most important thing right.

Archbishop: What do you mean?
What did they get right?
The Gray: Let me give you a few examples that you can easily understand?
a-The Gnostics said, Jesus is not divine; he is not the son of God. And, they got it right.
b-They said that Jesus was not crucified. And, they got it right.
c-The Gnositic books said that Jesus never came back from the dead and they got it right also.
And the greatest things about all of this the Gray's added, was when they said that the world (they meant Earth) and what is happening on Earth is not created by a good God but by an evil God; the devil himself.
The Grays explained that part of this belief is correct because Earth is where the lowest life-forms and brutal species live in the Universe. Galactic civilizations think Earth is a dumpster. This part is correct.
What they got wrong is that earth and its people were not created by evil and a vicious god, or by the devil himself, but by the Universe itself.
And, all those bad things happening in your society, nowadays, and in the past as well are because of your genes which were created by the Anunnaki.
Your final product was shaped in their image.
They should have said in the image of the Anunnaki, not the devil or an evil God, and they should have said (Repeated twice by the Gray) that the evil human race was created by the evil Anunnaki.

Archbishop: So you think the Church is dancing on the wrong foot?
The Gray: It is because of the Church and Organized Religions that your people never knew the truth.

Archbishop: Do you believe in God?
The Gray: According to the way you understand what God is or who is, each Universe has its own God.

The military men at the meeting got so bored and upset with these questions, because they didn't come to speak about Jesus, God, and such topics; rather, their interests where strictly in military areas, weapons and such, that they demanded he stop and not ask more questions.
The archbishop, who was furious, like an Irish apple, was so engrossed in his line of questioning that he simply insisted he maintain the control of the floor and continued, with the final blow.
But that wasn't the only blow, the more he listened to the demands to stop the more his face grew flushed, to the point that he couldn't control his flagellations; one after another, the questions weren't the only things he kept firing – it came from both ends.

The Lt Colonel sitting next to a general said, "Please sir, this is the time to fire your pipe and by all means blow it in my face. This guy's killing me." At that point the room had been stinking like a cemetery. And the whole time the Gray's sat there- unaware that there was a problem. Even worse, at one end, he was expelling like an old Ford model T, and on the other side he kept gripping the large gold cross that he wore around his neck, and rubbing it with a feverishly agitated motion, back and forth against his chest.
And the whole time, everyone was thinking what an interesting representation for a spiritual leader to demonstrate at one of the most important encounters with beings from another world, and an unprecedented meeting to ever occur in our planet's history.
And yet, across the table sat another very famous evangelist, who thankfully kept his dignified composure the entire meeting.

Archbishop: Well if you don't believe in God then who is keeping the Universe in order, keeping it running smoothly like a watch?
The Gray: This is a very wrong example because a watch needs to be rewound now and then.

If you don't, it will stop and you don't have the correct time. This means that what is behind the Universe is somebody who is re-winding it constantly.

And constantly does not mean hand, eyes and big white beard.

It is some sort of energy in the Universe, you can't understand now but it keeps the fabric of the Universe in place, and attached to itself.

Universal Energy and Dark Matter:
Years later the aliens explained to us what they meant by the "universal energy" that keeps the universe functioning properly and in order, since we didn't understand this concept in the 40's. When they met with us in the 70's, they explained to us what they meant by the "energy in the Universe"; they called it the Dark Matter or Dark Energy.

Nota bene: Abba Eban, Pope Pius XII and a German community in Argentina and Brazil: A few weeks following a very important meeting with the Grays "Greys" rumors spread the word that unauthorized copies of the transcripts were sent to Abba Eban, Pope Pius XII and a German community in Argentina and Brazil.

It was alleged that the Catholic archbishop supplied the Vatican with one set of the transcripts, and Jewish scientists who previously worked at Los Alamos and were present at the meeting, sent another set with a translation in Hebrew to Israel, and two protégés of Dr. von Braun sent a massive file to remnants of Nazis in South America.

The Library of the Vatican and the archives of the Observatory of the Vatican have an extensive library on extraterrestrials and their visits to Earth.

Cardinal Bertolli knew a lot about this.

*** *** ***

Pope Pius XII.

Abba Eban (Standing in the center) with US President Harry
Truman and Israeli Prime Minister Ben-Gurion.

Locations of negative energy on planet Earth:
The Aliens explained and pinpointed the locations of negative energy on planet Earth:
Note: Names of new countries and especially nations which did not exist back then, are intentionally added for correctness in geographical references. Several countries included in this section were not in existence yet, and/or had different names, at the time, meetings with aliens occurred during the forties, fifties, sixties, seventies, and even in recent years. Thus, I added their new names as they are known to us today. The following is a general representation and synopsis of the contents of the original transcripts.

The following is reproduced from 5 transcripts stretching over several years. Three of them were translated and re-translated into Russian, German and French. In recent years, almost all of the transcripts were translated to Hebrew; this was not a decision made by the military high command, but rather because of leaks from civilian scientists who were later called upon by the "big boss" to contribute their knowledge and expertise in the field.

At one of the meetings, civilian engineers and scientists asked the aliens if there is a science they could learn to properly forecast the weather, and/or to prevent natural catastrophes.
My personal belief is that they were not interested in meteorology, bur rather in developing a weapons system that could control and alter weather conditions.
They wanted to use the atmosphere, climate/whether as a weapon. Later, it became clear to me, that this was really what they wanted to know and accomplish. The topic of weather control and prediction led to the subject of Earth Energy.
A Harvard's scholar, and noted author, who at that time was known for a cult movement he created among his students, and who was experimenting with addictive/hallucinatory substances was present at one of the meetings.

He was particularly interested in the effect of gravity on humans and the underground energy currents' impact on human psyche, and mass behavior.

He kept asking lots of questions about aura, energy, and what he nicknamed "Underground Energy Flux".

Basically and primordially, what we have learned from those super intelligent non-human beings is this:

1. The globe is filled with a multitude of underground negative currents:

The globe is filled with a multitude of underground negative currents and spots that store and circulate negative energy.

The areas, spots, and zones that store negative energy (ies) are called Maraka Fasida.

And, they are almost everywhere underground. This was not something new to me. For the Anunnaki Ulema and Rouhaniyiin already told us that there are approximately 750,000 Maraka Fasida on planet Earth.

Many are unidentified and/or not revealed to us by the Masters. And, they have their own reasons for not telling us.

People who live above these negative zones (Spots and currents) will suffer enormously in their lives. And their suffering (Physical and mental) will encompass failure in business, relationships, entrepreneurial activities, partnerships, investments, health and mental development. Africa has the lion's share.

2. List of countries with considerable Maraka Fasida:

Africa

- Algeria (People's Democratic Republic of Algeria): 6
- Angola (Republic of Angola): 26
- Benin (Republic of Benin): 86
- Botswana (Republic of Botswana): 16
- Burkina Faso: 10
- Burundi (Republic of Burundi): 9
- Cameroon (Republic of Cameroon): 11
- Cape Verde (Republic of Cape Verde): 7

- Central African Republic (Central African Republic): 89
- Chad (Republic of Chad): 18
- Comoros (Union of the Comoros): 10
- Côte d'Ivoire (Republic of Côte d'Ivoire): 28
- Djibouti (Republic of Djibouti): 21
- Egypt (Arab Republic of Egypt): 10
- Equatorial Guinea (Republic of Equatorial Guinea): 96
- Eritrea (State of Eritrea): 26
- Ethiopia (Federal Democratic Republic of Ethiopia): 21
- Gabon (Gabonese Republic): 65
- Gambia (Republic of The Gambia): 74
- Ghana (Republic of Ghana): 91
- Guinea (Republic of Guinea): 94
- Guinea-Bissau (Republic of Guinea-Bissau): 26
- Kenya (Republic of Kenya): 98
- Lesotho (Kingdom of Lesotho): 26
- Liberia (Republic of Liberia): 315
- Libya (Great Socialist People's Libyan Arab Jamahiriya): 11
- Malawi (Republic of Malawi): 11
- Mali (Republic of Mali):21
- Mauritania (Islamic Republic of Mauritania): 21
- Morocco (Kingdom of Morocco): 9
- Mozambique (Republic of Mozambique): 39
- Namibia (Republic of Namibia): 21
- Niger (Republic of Niger): 89
- Nigeria (Federal Republic of Nigeria): 243
- Republic of the Congo (Republic of the Congo): 112
- Rwanda (Republic of Rwanda): 275
- Sao Tome and Principe: 78
- Senegal (Republic of Senegal): 76
- Seychelles (Republic of Seychelles): 43
- Sierra Leone (Republic of Sierra Leone): 348

- Somalia (Somali Republic): 721
- South Africa (Republic of South Africa): 154
- Sudan (Republic of Sudan): 19
- Swaziland (Kingdom of Swaziland): 19
- Tanzania (United Republic of Tanzania): 70
- Togo (Togolese Republic): 21
- Tunisia (Tunisian Republic): 9
- Uganda (Republic of Uganda): 121
- Western Sahara (Sahrawi Arab Democratic Republic): 19
- Zambia (Republic of Zambia): 32
- Zimbabwe (Republic of Zimbabwe): 98

Others:

Madagascar (Republic of Madagascar): 21
(Republic of Mauritius): 49

Africa's worst spots (Zones and currents) are located in:
In this order.
Sierra Leone (Republic of Sierra Leone).
Central African Republic (Central African Republic).
South Africa (Republic of South Africa).
Ghana (Republic of Ghana).
Nigeria (Federal Republic of Nigeria).
Rwanda (Republic of Rwanda).
Republic of the Congo (Republic of the Congo).
Uganda (Republic of Uganda).
Somalia (Somali Republic).

Europe

- Albania: 3
- Andorra: 3
- Armenia: 6
- Austria: 4

- Azerbaijan: 21
- Belarus: 6
- Belgium: 4
- Bosnia & Herzegovina: 11
- Bulgaria: 5
- Croatia: 13
- Cyprus: 6
- Czech Republic: 9
- Denmark: 3
- Estonia: 6
- Finland: 4
- France: 3
- Georgia: 4
- Germany: 9
- Greece: 9
- Hungary: 6
- Iceland: 3
- Ireland: 2
- Italy: 6
- Kosovo: 13
- Latvia: 3
- Liechtenstein: 1
- Lithuania: 4
- Luxembourg: 1
- Macedonia: 4
- Malta: 2
- Moldova: 2
- Monaco: 1
- Montenegro: 2
- The Netherlands: 3
- Norway: 2
- Poland: 4
- Portugal: 4
- Romania: 4
- Russia: 9
- San Marino: 1

- Serbia: 11
- Slovakia: 3
- Slovenia: 3
- Spain: 5
- Sweden: 1
- Switzerland: 1
- Turkey: 11
- Ukraine: 5
- United Kingdom: 6
- Vatican City (Holy See): 1

Europe's worst spots are located in:
In this order.

- Azerbaijan
- Croatia
- Kosovo
- Serbia
- Turkey
- Bosnia & Herzegovina
- Czech Republic
- Albania
- Andorra
- Russia
- Germany

Latin America and the Caribbeans

- Anguilla: 1
- Antigua and Barbuda: 1
- Argentina: 2
- Aruba: 1
- Bahamas: 5
- Barbados: 1
- Belize: 1

- Bermuda: 11
- Bolivia: 3
- Brazil: 3
- British Virgin Islands: 1
- Cayman Islands: 1
- Chile: 2
- Colombia: 6
- Costa Rica: 2
- Cuba: 3
- Dominican Republic: 3
- Ecuador: 2
- El Salvador: 2
- Grenada: 2
- Guatemala: 2
- Guyana: 4
- Haiti: 11
- Honduras: 2
- Jamaica: 6
- Mexico: 4
- Montserrat: 1
- Netherlands Antilles: 1
- Nicaragua: 2
- Panama: 2
- Paraguay: 2
- Peru: 2
- Saint Kitts and Nevis: 1
- Saint Lucia: 1
- Saint Vincent and the Grenadines: 1
- Suriname: 1
- Trinidad and Tobago: 1
- Turks and Caicos Islands: 1
- Uruguay: 1
- Venezuela: 1

Latin America and the Caribbeans worst spots are located in:

In this order.
- Haiti
- Bermuda
- Colombia
- Jamaica
- Bahamas
- Mexico
- Guyana

The United States

- Alabama: 4
- Alaska: 2
- American Samoa: 1
- Arizona: 3
- Arkansas: 2
- California: 7
- Colorado: 1
- Connecticut: 1
- Delaware: 1
- District of Columbia: 7
- Florida: 13
- Georgia: 2
- Guam: 1
- Hawaii: 3
- Idaho: 1
- Illinois: 2
- Indiana: 1
- Iowa: 1
- Kansas: 1
- Kentucky: 1
- Louisiana: 4
- Maine: 1
- Maryland: 2
- Massachussets: 2

- Michigan: 2
- Minnesota: 1
- Mississippi: 3
- Missouri: 2
- Montana: 1
- Nebraska: 1
- Nevada: 9
- New Hampshire: 1
- New Jersey: 3
- New Mexico: 2
- New York: 11
- North Carolina: 1
- North Dakota: 1
- Ohio: 2
- Oklahoma: 1
- Oregon: 1
- Pennsylvania: 2
- Puerto Rico: 4
- Rhode Island: 1
- South Carolina: 1
- South Dakota: 1
- Tennessee: 1
- Texas: 7
- Utah: 1
- Vermont: 1
- Virginia: 3
- Virgin Islands: 3
- Washington: 2
- West Virginia: 3
- Wisconsin: 3
- Wyoming: 1

United States' worst spots are located in (In this order)
Florida
New York
Nevada

Texas
California
District of Columbia
Louisiana
Alabama
Puerto Rico

In Canada: Canada has 3 spots.

Explanation:
A Delicate zone means one or all of the following:
1-The black dots refer to states, where the level and degree of your financial success and/or stability are pre-determined by circumstances and factors out of your control.
2-Although these states are not negative in etheric structure, the vibrations of their milieu (People living there, and underground currents) will affect the outcome of your efforts, planning, financial stability, and new enterprises.
This does not apply to all of us, but to some individuals who are "sensitive and sensible" to the underground negative spots and currents. Many people who live in some of these states succeeded beyond belief and became millionaires, while others failed miserably despite their hard work, intelligence and financial resources. California, New York and Greater Washington, DC (Including two areas in Maryland) are perfect examples.
You should consult your "Vibrations Personal Chart" and your Rizmanah.

New Jersey is a locale/Carrefour/conglomeration for conflicting currents, meaning unpredictable results. Consequently, if you have lived in neighboring areas where their Maraka Fasida are accentuated, then, you should not move your business, or start a new project in an area or zone situated above an underground negative current starting underground in New York. This is not financial advice I am giving you; and, you should not consider my explanation as a professional opinion. It is up to you, to consider the situation or disregard my argument.

Personally, I will not move my business and activities to any area, if it is directly linked to a negative current which originally starts and/or originates underground/spot/current of a state where the Maraka Fasida is strong.

From consulting my "Etheric Chart", I came to a conclusion that some streets and avenues in New York City will not be beneficial for a period of time starting in 2010 and ending in 2014. Again, this is my personal reading, and you should not categorically apply my findings to your personal situation. It is up to you.

But, if I were in your position, I would seriously consider these possibilities.

In New York:

- 19th Street between 7th Avenue and 8th Avenue is not a favorable spot.
- There are 2 blocks on 8th Avenue, considered to be extremely negative.
- 57th Street is not a beneficial etheric locale.
- 18th Street between 7th & 8th Avenue is not good spot for people who want to succeed in artistic careers, such as: acting, composing music and producing videos.
- On 23rd Street, near Chelsea Hotel, there are several bad luck pockets that could prevent many from having financial freedom. Many of the people living there will always struggle.
- Harlem area has 2 huge negative spots.
- 188th Street, in Inwood, is a good spot.
- However, there is one bad spot in Inwood above 200th Street, on the East side, zip code 10033 that has a few bad spots. Spiritual people can feel it as well as smell the bad vibes in the air. Its ramifications are stored in the walls of the buildings.
- Two particular areas in Park Slope, Brooklyn, are to be avoided. They are bad for business and they halt your creativity.
- There are delicate zones on 1st Avenue that could twist your luck.

- Some blocks of 1st Avenue could catapult your success, but you have to know upfront when you should get out of that area.
- Part of Binghamton has been affected by a negative underground current.

3-Some spots in delicate zones have a temporary effect, meaning that for a few months or a few years, your business, personal development, peace of mind and tranquility will not be negatively affected, but at some point, you should relocate to another area. Be alert, watch how things are going, revise your plans and compare results.

Create a time-table chart for all the results you are getting for a few months. Give yourself time, but observe very carefully how others who are conducting the same business are doing on a monthly basis.

Black line: Current of negative energy.
Explanation: The black line refers to a strong negative current. States located above this current are charged with Maraka Fasida strong vibrations. Florida takes the leads.
Bad spots in Florida:
- Miami Beach,
- Boca Raton,
- Delray Beach,
- Panama City,
- Kissimmee,
- Boynton Beach,
- Marathon.

In Washington, DC area (DC/Virginia/Maryland):
Bad spots in Virginia:
- Loudoun County,
- Leesburg,
- Tysons Corner.

Bad spots in Maryland:
- Columbia,

- Fell's Point.

Bad spots in Washington, DC:

- Two blocks on Wisconsin Avenue, North West,
- One block on M Street in Georgetown, North West,
- Brentwood,
- Capitol Hill,
- One block on Pennsylvania Avenue,
- Six blocks in the east/south areas.
- One huge bad spot on 14th Street.

Major currents (Spots and ramifications)

There are two major currents (Spots and ramifications) running underground in the United States. The first current is called Ishra-Tamam; it represents a positive energy. The second current is called Ishra-Atila; it represents a negative energy.

Who reviewed the Addendum to the transcripts?

Names of some scientists, military men and others who reviewed the Alien-Meeting transcripts and commented upon, (To name a few):

- General Kenney. Commander of the United States Strategic Air Forces
- Kenneth C. Royall. Special Assistant to the Secretary of War, 1945. Under Secretary of War, 1945-1947. Secretary of War, 1947. Secretary of the Army, 1947-1949
- Dr. Peter Goldmark (Péter Károly Goldmark). Scientist, inventor, and recipient of the National Medal of Science, awarded by President Carter
- General Curtis LeMay. Commander-in-Chief of the Strategic Air Command, from 1948 to 1957, and Vice Chief of Staff, U.S. Air Force, from 1957 to 1961
- Major General Clements McMullen. Commanding General of the San Antonio Air Materiel Area, Kelly Air Force Base, San Antonio, Texas
- Major General St. Clair Streett. Special assistant to the Commanding General, Air Materiel Command.

- John Bardeen. Physicist and inventor of the Transistor. He won twice the Noble Prize in Physics.
- Mr. Warren R. Austin
- Secretary of Defense, Forrestal
- Dr. W. Albert Noyes, President of the American Chemical Society
- Dr. Edward Teller, father of the H Bomb
- Dr. von Braun
- Dr. Enrico Fermi, winner of the Nobel Prize in physics. In 1938, Dr. Fermi was the world's greatest expert on neutrons
- Dr. Vannevar Bush. Vice-president and dean at MIT in 1932. President of Carnegie Institute in 1939. Chairman of the National Advisory Committee for Aeronautics. President Roosevelt appointed him Chairman of the National Defense Resource Committee (NDRC). FDR's senior military research advisor
- General Nathan F. Twining, United States Air Force Chief of Staff
- Lt. General Arthur Gilbert Trudeau, Chief of the Army's Research and Development Command
- Rear Admiral Roscoe H. Hillenkoetter, the first CIA Director, Director of the Central Intelligence Group, Member of the board of governors of the National Investigations Committee on Aerial Phenomena, etc.
- President George Bush, Sr.
- A scientist from Kelley-Koet Manufacturing Company, located in Kentucky

*** *** ***

Major General St. Clair Streett with General McMullen.

Major General Clements McMullen.

General Curtis LeMay

Secretary of War, Kenneth C. Royall.

John Bardeen. One of the most important physicists and inventors in American history.

Secretary of Defense, Forrestal shaking the hand of Admiral Byrd.

Lt. General Arthur Gilbert Trudeau.

Dr. Edward Teller, father of the H Bomb.

Dr. Enrico Fermi.

Dr. Vannevar Bush.

General Nathan F. Twining

Rear Admiral Roscoe H. Hillenkoetter.
First Director of the Central Intelligence Agency (CIA).

From L to R: Major General John Barclay, Dr. Von Braun. Barclay reviewed segments of the Aliens Transcripts.

Copies of the transcripts and reports:

- Transcripts sent in duplicate copies to The White House on Monday 9, February 1948.
- A synopsis of the transcripts (Heavily censored) sent to Dr. ...on Thursday 26, February 1948.
- A Top Secret Presidential Memorandum (Order) was issued on Wednesday 18, February 1948.
- A follow-up report was written and sent to The White House by Dr. Von Braun and Dr. Teller on Thursday 26, February 1948.

*** *** ***

Published by
Times Square Press
New York, Berlin
Website: www.timessquarepress.com

Printed in the
United States of America and Germany
2014